STUDENT LOANS

Who Borrows, and Why?

Joan Payne with Claire Callender

POLICY STUDIES INSTITUTE
London

The publishing imprint of the independent
POLICY STUDIES INSTITUTE
100 Park Village East, London NW1 3SR
Tel. 0171 468 0468   Fax. 0171 388 0914

ISBN 0 85374 728 8
PSI Report 848

PSI publications are available from:
Grantham Book Services, Isaac Newton Way
Alma Park Industrial Estate, Grantham, Lincs.
Fax.   01476 541061
Tel.   01476 541080

Typesetting by PCS Mapping and DTP, Newcastle upon Tyne
Printed in Great Britain by Page Bros (Norwich) Ltd

Contents

Tables and Figures

Acronyms and Abbreviations

DfEE   Department for Education and Employment
DipHE   Diploma in Higher Education
ELB   Education and Library Board
HE   Higher Education
HESA   Higher Education Statistics Agency Ltd
LEA   Local Education Authority
NOP   National Opinion Polls
PGCE   Post-Graduate Certificate in Education
PSI   Policy Studies Institute
SAAS   Student Awards Agency for Scotland
SEG   Socio-Economic Group
SOED   Scottish Office Education and Industry Department
UFC   Universities' Funding Council

Acknowledgements and Disclaimer

This report is based on data from the 1996 Student Income and Expenditure Survey. This survey was funded by the Department for Education and Employment, the fieldwork was carried out by National Opinion Polls (NOP), and the initial computer analysis was performed by Karen Mackinnon of the Policy Studies Institute (PSI). The present analysis was also funded by the Department for Education and Employment (DfEE), and we thank the Steering Group for their advice, constructive criticism and support. Any mistakes in the analysis are of course our own. The views expressed in the report are the authors' and do not necessarily reflect those of the DfEE.

Executive Summary

Introduction

Student loans were introduced in 1990, with the aim of shifting part of the costs of student support in higher education from the state and from parents to students. By the mid-1990s, maximum loans were only a little less than the maximum (means-tested) basic maintenance grant. Loans were not means-tested and were interest-free in real terms. In 1995/96, 59 per cent of eligible students took out a student loan. Repayments started when income exceeded 85 per cent of national average earnings, but were not otherwise related to earnings, and loans normally had to be repaid within five years.

Under proposals announced by the new Labour Government in July 1997 that affect new students starting their courses in 1998/99 or later, the remaining maintenance grants for lower income families will be replaced by loans of the same value. Tuition fees will be introduced for all but the poorest students, and for higher income families an additional maintenance loan will be available equivalent to the tuition fee. In addition, the arrangements for repaying loans will be changed. The level of income at which repayments become due will be raised, and repayments will be income contingent and spread out over a longer period.

Student loans are thus set to become an even bigger element in student funding, and it is important to understand their impact on students. The main aim of the present study is to develop statistical models of the factors related to the probability of taking out a student loan. We also consider the amount borrowed, and the reasons that students give for their decisions.

The data come from the 1996 Student Income and Expenditure Survey, which is a cross-sectional study of a nationally representative random sample of full-time home students in higher education in the United Kingdom, on courses attracting loans and mandatory awards. A total of 1971 students in 72 institutions were interviewed in spring 1996, representing a response rate of 59 per cent.

The next two sections of this summary describe the basic model of loan take-up and an extended model with additional predictor variables. This is followed by findings from the model for the amount borrowed. The penultimate section deals with students' reasons for their decisions about loans, while the final section discusses some implications of this research.

Basic Model

The first model related to the take-up of student loans during the academic year 1995/96, and was confined to predictor variables which were more likely to represent influences on the loan decision than to represent consequences of that decision. The following findings hold true after allowances have been made for a range of relevant factors.

Women were less likely to take out a student loan than men. This may reflect gender differences in attitudes to debt.

Asian students were substantially less likely to take out student loans than members of other ethnic groups. Sample numbers were too small to be sure of the reasons for this, though it may be linked to lack of knowledge about student loans.

Second and third year students on three year courses were more likely to take out a student loan than first year students. This was partly because first years were more likely to draw on savings and were more likely to live in comparatively cheap college-provided accommodation. Students on one-year courses were even less likely to take out a loan than students in the first year of a three-year course. For students on courses lasting four years or longer, the likelihood of taking out a loan increased with each subsequent year of study.

Whether or not students lived with a partner made no difference to the likelihood of taking out a student loan. Having dependent children may possibly have increased take-up, and students who were lone parents had a high take-up rate.

Until they were in their late 20s, their likelihood of taking out a student loan increased with the age at which students started their courses. One reason for this was that the older students were when they started their courses, the less parents tended to contribute to their support.

Take-up of student loans was higher in the age group 25–29 than any other age group, but from age 30 onwards, take-up declined. This fall could not be explained by a greater use of savings, by bigger part-time or casual earnings, by more employer sponsorship, or by a greater use of commercial credit. It may be explained by the fact that financial help from partners increased with age, or it may indicate that older students expected a lower financial return to their qualifications than younger students.

Although student loans were not means-tested, the likelihood of taking out a loan increased with the size of the means-tested maintenance grant awarded to the student. For students under 25, the latter was a good indicator of family socio-economic circumstances. Among mature students, those with small grants had take-up rates as high as those with big grants, though take-up rates were lower among students with no grant at all.

The decision about whether to take out a loan is likely to be influenced by expected future earnings, but unfortunately the data contain no direct measure of these. Possible, though inadequate, proxies are the status of the higher education institution that the student attended and the subject studied. However, no association was found between either of these variables and loan take-up.

No evidence was found of any variation in loan take-up between the regions in which the institutions of higher education were located.

Most of these results were confirmed by a second model for loan take-up at any time during the course up until the time of interview, rather than just during the academic year 1995/96.

Model with Additional Predictor Variables

The third model related to taking out a loan during 1995/96. It included the predictor variables discussed so far, and added in further variables whose relationship with take-up was ambiguous. By this we mean that causality could run in either or both directions, or indeed that the variable and loan take-up may have been associated only as the joint outcome of some third prior factor. The interpretation of the following results is thus uncertain.

Students who lived at home were less likely to take out a student loan than students living in college accommodation. The latter group was in turn less likely to take out loans than students living in accommodation that they rented or owned independently.

The greater the amount of money provided by parents, the less likely students were to take out a loan. This is after taking into account the size of the maintenance grant, which was itself related to the contribution that parents were expected to make.

Students who had borrowed from commercial sources were more likely than other students to take out a student loan, and this likelihood increased with the size of the commercial debts.

Students who did paid work during term-time had higher loan take-up rates than other students. This relationship became weaker when the level of the students' 'non-essential' expenditure was taken into account.

The biggest element in 'essential' expenditure related to accommodation costs, so once type of accommodation was included in the model, 'essential' expenditure had no further relationship with loan take-up. However the level of 'non-essential' expenditure was strongly correlated with take-up. When we controlled for the level of 'non-essential' expenditure, the difference in take-up between students in college-provided accommodation and students who rented or owned independently disappeared. This suggests that the high rates of loan take-up among students in independent accommodation were linked with higher expenditure on other items.

The less that students knew about how student loans worked, the less likely they were to take out a loan. Once the level of knowledge about loans was included in the model, the difference in take-up rates between white and Asian students lost its significance, indicating that Asian students' low rates of take-up may have been associated with an imperfect understanding of student loans.

Models for the Amount Borrowed

The maximum loan that students could take out depended on whether they lived with their parents during term, whether they were studying in London or elsewhere, and whether they were in their final year. Nearly nine out of ten borrowers took out the maximum for which they were eligible, which made it hard to develop a good statistical model. The following findings are therefore only tentative.

There was some indication that borrowers in their final year, when maximum loans were smaller, may have been more likely to borrow the maximum than students in earlier years.

Borrowers on courses lasting more than three years may have been less likely to take out the maximum loan than borrowers on shorter courses.

Borrowers with no maintenance grant and borrowers with large grants may have been more likely to take out the maximum loan than borrowers with small grants.

Borrowers with a partner in a relatively well paid job may have been less likely to take out the maximum loan than other borrowers.

Borrowers with a low level of knowledge about student loans may have been less likely to take out the maximum loan than borrowers who were well informed.

Reasons for Borrowing and Not Borrowing

More than three in four borrowers said that their main reason for taking out a student loan was financial need, while one in seven referred to the financial advantages of loans. Nearly two in three non-borrowers cited concerns about borrowing as their main reason for not taking out a loan, while one in four said they had no financial need to borrow.

Men were more likely than women to cite financial advantages as their main reason for taking out a loan, while women were more likely than men to say that they had not got a loan because of concerns about borrowing.

Students aged 20 or over at the start of their course were more likely than younger students to cite 'financial need' as their reason for getting a loan. In addition, the further on students were in their course, the more likely they were to cite financial need as their main reason for borrowing.

Borrowers with no maintenance grant were less likely to cite financial need than borrowers with large grants.

Discussion

When interpreting these findings, it is important to bear in mind the following limitations of the analysis:

- it relates to the funding structures in place up until the recently announced changes; the abolition of maintenance grants and introduction of tuition fees is likely to change the picture;
- the maximum student loan debt that students in our sample could incur was smaller than the size of potential debts for subsequent cohorts of students, and much smaller than the debts that future cohorts of students are likely to incur;
- we have no data on expected future earnings, which we would expect to influence loan decisions;
- we lack the longitudinal data that are needed to clarify the causal relationships underlying several of the associations we have found.

Because students from poorer families incur bigger debts than students from more prosperous backgrounds, the fear of debt might deter some young people from poorer families from entering higher education. Some commentators suggest that the potential deterrent effects of the loans system might be reduced if repayments were tied more closely to income, and this forms part of the government's proposed changes.

The loans system is of particular benefit to students who do not receive the assessed parental contribution to maintenance. One in six students whose parents were expected to contribute faced this problem, which was most severe in the 20–24 age group.

Some well-off students took out student loans because of the financial advantages of their zero real interest rate. If loans were subject to commercial rates of interest, there would be less incentive to take out a loan for reasons other than financial need.

Students who were lone parents had particularly severe financial difficulties and were more likely to take out loans than others. Education has a special role for lone parents as a route out of dependence on state benefits, and their financial problems deserve attention.

Some students – especially women – appear to be averse to the idea of debt, however economically rational it may be to take out a loan, and others may be deterred from entering higher education for this reason. This raises the question of whether such young people should be encouraged to change their attitudes, or whether this would promote a culture unworried by debt.

| Introduction

The Student Loans Scheme

Up until 1990, when student loans were introduced, students in higher education in Britain were largely financed by government-funded awards covering both tuition fees and living costs, or maintenance. All eligible students on 'designated' courses – courses leading to a first degree, to a diploma of comparable standard, or to a Post-Graduate Certificate in Education (PGCE) – received mandatory awards. These covered full payment of tuition fees, plus a maintenance grant whose size depended on the income of the student's parents or spouse. Discretionary awards were also available for students who attended certain other courses, or who were not personally eligible.[1]

This system of mandatory and discretionary grants was introduced in 1962, when less than 6 per cent of the relevant age group entered higher education. However, rapid growth in the number of students in full-time higher education during the 1960s and again in the late 1980s and early 1990s meant that the cost of student support has escalated greatly. Following a 1988 White Paper, the student loans scheme was introduced in 1990 in order to contain the costs of student support without curtailing the expansion of higher education.[2]

The basic aim of the student loans scheme was to move part of the financial burden of higher education from the state and parents to the student. The justification for this move was that not only did students

---

1. Personal eligibility depends on length of residence in the British Islands and previous participation in higher education.
2. The relevant acts were the 1990 Education (Student Loans) Act and the 1990 Education (Student Loans) (Northern Ireland) Order. The rationale for the legislation was set out in the White Paper *Top-Up Loans for Students* (Department of Education and Science 1988).

receive a substantial return to higher education in terms of increased future earnings, but that the rate of return to the student – the 'private' rate of return – was higher than the return to the economy as a whole, or the 'social' rate of return.[3] This was because tuition was free to the student, and maintenance was heavily subsidised.

The government's intention in introducing student loans was to reduce students' reliance on maintenance grants as their major source of income, while establishing student loans as a significant supplementary source of income. To achieve this, maintenance grants were frozen at their level for the 1990/91 academic year. As the real value of maintenance grants was eroded by inflation, the deficit was to be made up by an increase in the value of student loans, and this process was intended to continue until loans and grants were equal in value. In 1994, this equalisation process was accelerated, and by 1996/97 the maximum student loans available were broadly equal to the maximum basic maintenance grant.

Under the scheme introduced in 1990, loans were not means-tested, which meant that all eligible students on designated courses could apply, regardless of their family income. Borrowers usually started to repay their loans in the April after they completed their course. However, if their income did not exceed 85 per cent of national average earnings, they could apply to defer repayments. Unless repayment was deferred, loans normally had to be repaid within five years. For most borrowers, an outstanding loan was cancelled after 25 years, or when the borrower reached the age of 50, whichever was earlier (provided that they were not in arrears or in default). Interest on loans was linked to inflation, as measured by the Retail Price Index, so that, in real terms, loans were interest-free.

The academic year 1995/96 was the sixth year of operation of the student loans scheme. In that year, 'full-year' student loans accounted for between 41 and 42 per cent of the total resources available to mandatory award holders in the UK.[4] 560,000 students received a loan, representing 59 per cent of those estimated to be eligible. Total loan payments

---

3. Current DfEE estimates suggest that the private rate of return to a degree is around 11–14 per cent, while the social rate of return is around 7–9 per cent (Steel and Sausman, 1996).
4. The maximum loan for students in the final year of their course was less than for other students, as the loan was not intended to cover the summer vacation. Loans for students not in their final year were termed 'full-year' loans as they covered the summer vacation. See Chapter 4 for more information on the maximum amounts that could be borrowed.

amounted to £700.8 million, with an average value for each loan of £1,252. More than two-fifths of students liable for repayments had been granted deferment because their income was below the repayment threshold, which in 1995/96 was £15,204 per annum. Repayments from those due to repay amounted to £65.8 million.[5]

In July 1997, in response to Sir Ron Dearing's National Committee of Inquiry into Higher Education (DfEE 1997a), the new Labour Government announced substantial changes to the system of student funding (DfEE 1997b). These changes will affect new students starting their courses in 1998/9 or later. The remaining maintenance grants are to be discontinued, and for lower income families will be replaced by loans of the same value. A tuition fee of £1,000 will be charged, although the poorest students will be exempted. For higher income families, an additional maintenance loan will be made available equivalent to the tution fee.

While the proportion of student funding coming from loans will be increased, steps will be taken to limit the burden of repayments. Repayments will be contingent upon income, and typical repayment periods are expected to be longer than under the present system. Some special measures are also directed at students who may have particular difficulties: supplementary hardship loans of £250 per year and non-means tested specific grants for students with special needs. There will be special arrangements for students entering teacher training and some health and social care professional courses.

The Present Study

These changes mean that student loans will become the major vehicle for government funding for student support. It is therefore very important to understand the impact loans have had on students.

The main aim of the present study is therefore to develop a statistical model of the factors related to the probability of taking out a student loan. We also examine the factors relating to the amount borrowed, and the reasons that students give for their decision to borrow or not.

The importance of forecasting future take-up means we have to be clear about the causal relationship between take-up and the factors corre-

---

5. All the statistics in this paragraph are taken from Department for Education and Employment (1996).

lated with take-up. Some factors may be correlated with loan take-up only because they themselves result from a prior decision to take out a loan, and are of little use in forecasting. Unfortunately, for many of the variables which are correlated with take-up, it is impossible to determine from the data currently available the extent to which they are determinants or consequences of the loan decision. This ambiguity affects not only subjective characteristics such as students' knowledge about loans and their attitudes to debt in general, but also many objective characteristics. For example, students may choose to live with parents during term, or to apply only to institutions outside London, in order to reduce expenses and so avoid the need to take out a loan.

Because of this problem, the main analysis of student loan take-up is divided into two stages. In the first stage (Chapter 2) the choice of predictor variables is confined to those whose causal relationship with take-up is relatively unambiguous. Note the qualification 'relatively', for there are very few factors (apart perhaps from gender and ethnicity) which could not possibly be affected by a prior decision about taking out a student loan. For example, students might choose to defer entry to university for a year or two in order to build up savings and avoid going into debt, or they might reject the idea of a four-year course because they wish to limit their potential debt. In the absence of longitudinal data, the best that can be claimed for the factors discussed in Chapter 2 is that it seems more likely that they preceded rather than followed the loan decision. The second stage of the analysis (Chapter 3) explores other factors associated with loan take-up where it is very plausible that causality might run in either, or even both, directions.

While Chapters 2 and 3 are concerned simply with whether students took out a student loan or not, Chapter 4 looks at the amount they borrowed. A model is presented for whether or not students took out the maximum loan for which they were eligible.

Chapter 5 looks at the determinants of loan take-up from the student's point of view. It examines the reasons that students gave for deciding to take out a student loan, or for deciding not to do so, and shows how these reasons differ between different groups of students. In so doing, it sheds further light on the results of the statistical models.

Finally, Chapter 6 summarises the main results and suggests some possible implications for government policy on student loans.

The Student Income and Expenditure Survey

The analysis is based on the 1996 Student Income and Expenditure Survey. This is a cross-sectional study of a nationally representative stratified random sample of students in higher education institutions in the United Kingdom, on courses attracting loans and mandatory awards. This includes courses leading to a first degree, a Diploma in Higher Education (DipHE), a Higher National Diploma (HND) or a Postgraduate Certificate in Education (PGCE). The study was confined to students on these courses who were eligible for mandatory awards and loans, that is, they were full-time students who were ordinarily resident in the United Kingdom. Students on sandwich courses who had earned money from paid placement work during the academic year in which they were interviewed were excluded.

The survey was carried out by personal interview between February and May 1996, with the majority of interviews (58 per cent) taking place in March. A total of 1971 students were interviewed in 72 institutions, representing a response rate of 59 per cent. Second- and third-year students, students at London institutions and mature students were deliberately over-sampled so that sample numbers would be large enough for their finances to be examined in detail. A weighting matrix was constructed to correct population estimates for this over-sampling, though no correction was made for possible response bias. Full details of the survey methodology can be found in Callender and Kempson, 1996.

The survey asked students whether they had taken out a student loan during the current academic year, that is, during 1995/96. The present analysis is concerned only with the determinants of loans from the Student Loans Company, not loans from other sources, such as bank loans or private loans. Respondents were classed as having taken out a student loan if they had received a loan at any time since the start of the academic year, or if they had applied for one and were awaiting payment. They were classed as not having taken out a student loan if they said that they intended to do so but had not yet applied. On this definition, the proportion of students taking out a student loan was 54 per cent using weighted data (55 per cent using unweighted data).

As student loans could be taken out at any time during the academic year, the question arises of how representative these 54 per cent were of all students taking out loans. Figure 1.1 shows that in fact most loans were taken out relatively early in the year. By the end of March 1996, the month

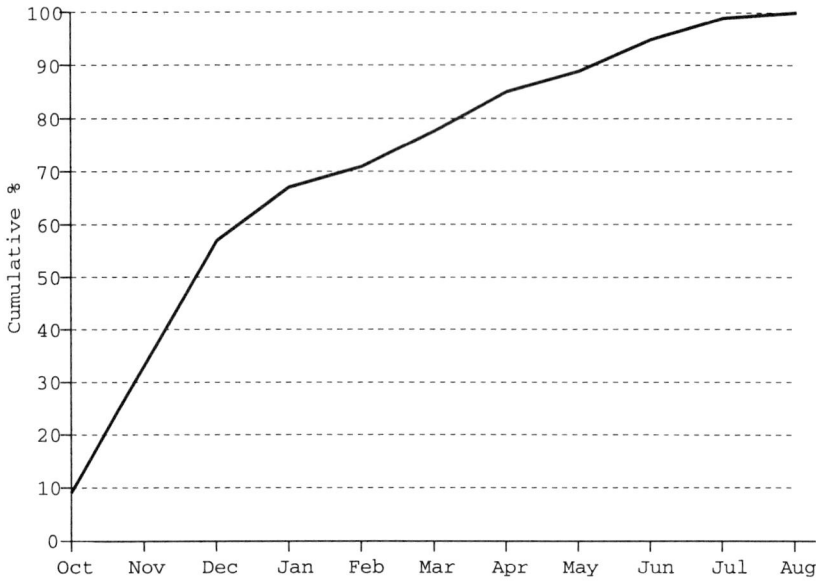

Source: Student Loans Company (authors' calculations).

Figure 1.1 *Award of student loans by month, 1995/96*
(cumulative percentage of 1995/96 total)

in which most survey interviews were conducted, nearly four-fifths of the total number of loans given during 1995/96 had been awarded. As our figures (unlike those in Figure 1.1) include students who had applied for loans but not yet received them, they are likely to represent an even larger proportion of the annual total. Calculated another way, with total take-up for 1995/96 standing at 59 per cent of those eligible,[6] our 54 per cent represents more than nine out of ten students taking out loans during 1995/96.

Students were also asked if they had any outstanding debts to the Student Loans Company from loans taken out in previous academic years. Adding in outstanding debts raised the total proportion of students with a student loan to 61 per cent (61 per cent also unweighted).

---

6.   Department for Education and Employment (1996).

Modelling Procedures

As much of the information collected in the Student Income and Expenditure Survey relates specifically to the academic year in which it took place (1995/96), this report concentrates on loans taken out during that academic year. However models are also given for whether students had ever taken out a loan during their course.

All the models presented here are logistic models, and model estimates are reported in their exponentiated form, as multiplicative effects on the odds of taking out a loan. For readers who are unfamiliar with the logistic model, Annex A explains how to interpret the estimates, and how significance testing is carried out.[7]

The models are parsimonious, in that all the predictor variables significantly improve model fit. There is one exception to this: the location of the institution where the student was based was not significant as a predictor of the likelihood of taking out a loan, but was included in the models for the technical reason that it was one of three variables used to construct the weighting matrix.[8] The other two variables involved in the weighting matrix – age at the start of the course and year of study – were significant predictors in their own right. As all three of the weighting variables were fitted as predictor variables in the models, it was not necessary to weight the data in order to get unbiased results.

The sample numbers on which the models were based were a little smaller than the total number of survey respondents because not all respondents gave information on whether they had taken out a loan.[9]

---

7.   For further information on the logistic model, see Cox and Snell (1989). The models were fitted using the GLIM statistical package (Francis, Green and Payne 1993).

8.   See the section above on 'Data'.

9.   There was information on whether students had ever taken out a loan for 1,950 survey respondents, and on whether they had taken out a loan in the current academic year for 1,945 respondents.

Chapter 2 | Models for Loan Take-up: Stage One

Model 1: Taking out a Student loan in the Current Academic Year

In this chapter we construct a model for the take-up of student loans using predictor variables that were relatively unambiguous in terms of their causal relationship with take-up. We concentrate first on modelling take-up during the academic year 1995/96, the year in which the data were collected, and to which many of the survey questions relate. Later in the chapter, we also present a model for taking out a loan at any time during the student's course up to and including the year of the survey.

As Callender and Kempson (1996) have already shown through cross-tabular analysis, the proportion of students who took out a student loan during the first half of the academic year 1995/96 varied between different groups of students. Table 2.1 shows the variables that remained significant after taking into account the effects of other factors. Two slightly different versions of the model are presented: version A fits just the 'main' effects of the predictor variables, while version B includes interactions between predictor variables. We focus first on version A (Model 1A in Table 2.1).

This model confirms that men were more likely to take out a loan than women even when other differences between the sexes were taken into account. This effect was quite large and statistically highly significant. It is hard to say whether a rational calculation of economic self-interest would produce this outcome. Women's earnings are on average smaller than men's, but, under the rules in force at the time of the survey, once income had reached the repayment threshold of 85 per cent of national

Table 2.1 *Models for taking out a student loan in the academic year 1995/96 (excluding causally ambiguous predictors)*

	Model 1A estimate	Model 1B estimate
Constant	0.63	0.62
Gender:		
Male	1.00	1.00
Female	****0.70	****0.70
Ethnic identification:		
White	1.00	1.00
Black Caribbean, Black African, Black other	0.97	1.03
Asian (Indian, Pakistani, Bangladeshi, Chinese)	****0.40	****0.41
Other	1.83	1.77
Course length and year of study:		
1st year of a 3 year course	1.00	1.00
2nd year of a 3 year course	**1.45	**1.43
3rd year of a 3 year course	***1.53	***1.52
1 year course	**0.33	**0.34
1st year of a 2 year course	1.56	1.49
2nd year of a 2 year course	1.10	1.14
1st year of 4+ year course	0.71	0.71
2nd year of 4+ year course	0.99	0.98
3rd year of 4+ year course	0.99	0.90
4th or higher year of 4+ year course	1.27	1.27
Family situation:		
No partner and no dependent children	1.00	1.00
Has partner but no dependent children	1.12	1.06
Has partner and dependent child(ren)	1.56	1.32
Has dependent child(ren) but no partner	***3.22	***2.77
Location of HE institution:		
UK excluding Greater London	1.00	1.00
Greater London	0.87	0.81
Age at start of course:		
18	1.00	–
16–17	0.68	–
19	**1.32	–
20	*1.43	–
21	1.50	–
22–24	1.14	–
25–29	***2.02	–
30–34	*1.69	–
35 and over	1.08	–

continued

Table 2.1 *continued*

	Model 1A estimate	Model 1B estimate
Value of maintenance grant for 1995/96 (inc allowances):		
£0 (30% of sample)	1.00	–
£1–£796 (4th decile)	*1.41	–
£797–£1382 (5th decile)	***1.78	–
£1383–£1650 (6th decile)	1.14	–
£1651–£1872 (7th decile)	****2.95	–
£1873–£1976 (8th decile)	****2.73	–
£1977–£2340 (9th decile)	****2.88	–
£2341 or more (10th decile)	***2.00	–
No information	***2.11	–
Age at start of course combined with value of maintenance grant:		
Age 18; no grant	–	1.00
Age 18; £1–£1650 (deciles 4–6)	–	**1.52
Age 18; £1651 or more (deciles 7–10)	–	***2.84
Age 19; no grant	–	1.38
Age 19; £1–£1650 (deciles 4–6)	–	**1.67
Age 19; £1651 or more (deciles 7–10)	–	****3.83
Age 20–24; no grant	–	*1.59
Age 20–24; £1–£1650 (deciles 4–6)	–	1.34
Age 20–24; £1651 or more (deciles 7–10)	–	****4.06
Age 25+; no grant	–	1.22
Age 25+; £1–£1650 (deciles 4–6)	–	****3.70
Age 25+; £1651 or more (deciles 7–10)	–	****3.72
All aged <18, regardless of size of grant	–	1.11
All with no data on size of grant	–	****2.68
N (unweighted)	*1945*	*1945*
Scaled deviance	*2463*	*2472*
Residual df	*1911*	*1914*

Significance levels: * 10%, ** 5%, *** 1%, **** 0.1%.

Table 2.2 *Percentage of students taking out a student loan in the academic year 1995/96, by gender and age at start of course*

	Men		Women	
	% of group	*weighted N*	*% of group*	*weighted N*
Age 16–18	50	408	43	504
Age 19	62	180	49	197
Age 20–24	62	181	55	152
Age 25 and over	70	152	69	172
All age groups	58	921	50	1025

average earnings, the size of repayments was unaffected by income level. Thus on average, repayments formed a larger share of women's incomes, and this may have acted as a disincentive for them, as also for other students whose expected future earnings were around or a little below the national average. On the other hand, liability for repayments was based solely on the student's own income, and the income of a spouse or partner was not taken into account. As women were more likely than men to have a period of economic inactivity within a few years of leaving higher education in order to bring up children, they were more likely than men to benefit from deferred repayments.

Another possible explanation for the sex difference in loan take-up is that women students, especially mature women students, may have been more likely than men to receive financial support from a partner. However, as we shall see later, partnership status was not a significant predictor of loan take-up in itself, but only became significant in combination with the presence of dependent children. Moreover, as Table 2.2 shows, the gender difference in take-up was only found for students who were under 25 at the start of their course, whereas financial support from a partner was more common amongst mature students.

In fact, the group that Table 2.2 shows to be least likely to take out a loan – women students aged under 19 at the start of their course – had a lower total income from sources other than loans than any other group defined by age and gender. This is shown in Table 2.3. Indeed, women's mean non-loan income was lower than men's in all age groups apart from age 25 and over. If the decision about whether or not to take out a loan were driven mainly by financial need, these figures would lead us to

Table 2.3 *Mean total income* excluding student loans in the academic year 1995/96, by gender and age at start of course*

	Men		Women	
	mean income	weighted N	mean income	weighted N
Age 16–18	£3945	390	£3790	480
Age 19	£4322	175	£3916	192
Age 20–24	£4052	173	£3866	152
Age 25 and over	£5180	145	£6521	166
All age groups	£4244	883	£4285	990

* Including both maintenance grants and income from other sources.

Note: Excludes those with missing information on income.

expect women to be more likely to take out loans than men. The fact that the reverse holds true suggests that the gender difference in loan take-up may be in part a reflection of more deep-rooted gender differences, or of cultural and family pressures. In particular, women may tend to be more cautious than men, and may also manage better on a small income than men generally do. This interpretation is supported by the fact that a dislike of borrowing and reluctance to take on debt was cited more often than 'not needing the money' by students who had not taken out a loan as their reason for not borrowing.[10]

Ethnic identification also proved to be a highly significant predictor of take-up in Model 1A, with Asian students (those describing themselves as Indian, Pakistani, Bangladeshi or Chinese) much less likely to take out a loan than other groups. However there appeared to be no difference between white and black students. As all the students included in the Student Income and Expenditure Survey were UK domiciled and eligible for loans, the explanation for this ethnic difference must be sought in cultural factors. One part of the explanation may be that some Asian students had lifestyles that involved lower expenditure, particularly perhaps on entertainments such as pubs, clubs and discos. Another part of the explanation may be that some Muslim students had religious objections to borrowing money on which interest was charged.

---

10. Callender and Kempson (1996), Chapter 4. See Chapter 5 for a fuller discussion of reasons for taking out and not taking out loans.

Table 2.4 *Use of savings by year of study: students on three year courses only*

	% drawing on savings	Weighted N	Mean sum withdrawn	Weighted N
First-year students	51	364	£703	184
Second-year students	38	375	£720	144
Third-year students	43	436	£660	187
All students on 3 year courses	44	1175	£692	515

Unfortunately in the present study sample numbers for Asian students were too small to explore these hypotheses further.[11]

Course length and year of study are logically connected (for example, it is impossible to be in the fourth year of a three-year course), and so a composite variable was constructed combining the two. Three-fifths of students in the survey were on three-year courses, and Model 1A shows that these were more likely to take out a loan in the second or third year of the course than in their first year. One reason for this is that first-year students were more likely than students in their second or third years to draw on savings, as Table 2.4 shows. Presumably, by the second and third years of the course, savings were more likely to be exhausted. We shall see below in Chapter 3 that the type of accommodation in which students lived was also an important factor in explaining why second-and third-year students were more likely to take out loans than first-years.

The model results show that students on one-year courses were much less likely to take out a loan even than students in the first year of a three-year course. Most students on one-year courses who were eligible for student loans were studying for a PGCE. In the Student Income and Expenditure Survey, PGCE students were classed as being on a one-year course if there was a gap of at least one academic year between completing their first degree and starting the PGCE course, but if there was no such gap, they were classed as being in their fourth year of study. Thus students on one-year courses were much more likely than students

---

11. There is evidence that members of the wider Asian community in Britain make relatively little use of sources of credit outside of their family and friends, and know relatively little about commercial schemes. See Herbert and Kempson 1996.

on longer courses to have been in paid work in the year before their course began, and so had more opportunity to accumulate savings.[12]

In contrast to students on three-year courses, students in the second year of a two-year course appeared not more, but less likely to borrow than first-year students, though the difference was not statistically significant. The lack of significance may simply have been due to small sample numbers.[13] However students on two-year courses were distinctive in many respects: five in six were studying for an HND, 19 out of 20 attended 'new' universities (ie those which up until the early 1990s were polytechnics or other non-university higher education institutions) or institutions which did not have university status, and nearly two-thirds were clustered in just three subject areas, namely business and administrative studies, computing and the creative arts. They also tended to be older than other students, and so were more likely to have been in employment before enrolling on their course.[14] It is therefore perhaps not surprising that their pattern of borrowing should be different from other students.

For students on courses lasting four or more years, the likelihood of taking out a loan was not significantly different in any year of study, when they were compared with students in the first year of a three-year course.[15] However, the likelihood did appear to increase with year of study. If we re-fit Model 1A, taking students in the first year of a four-year or longer course as the reference category on which comparisons are based, we find that students in their fourth or higher year of study were in fact significantly more likely to take out a loan than students in the first year of a long course.

Our model shows that students who lived with a partner but had no dependent children were no more likely to take out a loan than students who had neither a partner nor dependent children. For students who had both a partner and dependent children the likelihood of taking out a loan

---

12. Sample numbers for students on one year courses were very small (39 unweighted). However, 49 per cent of this group drew on savings, compared to 43 per cent of students on longer courses.
13. The unweighted number of students in the sample on two year courses is 89.
14. 25 per cent of students on two-year courses were aged under 19 at the start of their course compared to 43 per cent of the sample as a whole. However the proportion of students on two-year courses who drew on savings (42 per cent) was very similar to the proportion amongst students on three-year courses.
15. Sample numbers are ample for any differences to reach statistical significance: in total, 694 respondents (unweighted) were on courses lasting four or more years.

was estimated to be greater, but the difference still did not reach significance. However students who had no partner but who had dependent children were much more likely to take out a loan than other students.[16] The reasons for this seem fairly obvious: families with dependent children have greater outgoings than other students, and lone parents are less likely to receive financial help from their children's other parent than parents who live with a partner.

In Chapter 1 we explained the technical reasons why the model includes a variable indicating whether the student's institution was located in Greater London.[17] This variable had no significant effect on the likelihood of taking out a loan during 1995/96.

The model estimates for the student's age at the start of the course showed, with one exception, a steady increase from age 16–17 up to age 25–29 in the likelihood of taking out a loan.[18] One reason for this is that, up to the age of 25, the older the student, the less generous parents appeared to be in the financial support they provided. Table 2.5 shows that, amongst students whose parents were assessed for a contribution towards their maintenance, 51 per cent of those aged under 19 at the start of their course expected to be given more than the assessed contribution. The same was true of 46 per cent of those aged 19 at the start of their course, and 38 per cent of those aged 20 to 24. Conversely, 15 per cent of those aged 19 or under at the start of the course expected to receive less than the assessed contribution, compared to 24 per cent of those aged 20 to 24.

Students were much less likely to receive additional financial help from their parents if they lived with their families during term-time than if they lived elsewhere. 21 per cent of students living with their family expected to get more than the assessed parental contribution to their maintenance and 34 per cent expected to get less than the assessed contribution, compared to 54 per cent and 13 per cent respectively among students living elsewhere. As younger students were the group most likely to be living with their parents,[19] it follows that the age of the

---

16. Not all these students were lone parents, as the classification includes students whose children were living apart from them. The term 'partner' here includes both cohabitees and spouses.
17. See page 7.
18. The exception was in the age band 22–24. This may have been a chance fluctuation.
19. See Table 3.2 in Chapter 3.

Table 2.5 *Student expectations about the assessed parental contribution towards maintenance (students whose parents were assessed and expected to make a contribution)*

| | Age at start of course | | | Total |
| | under 19 | 19 | 20–24 | under 25 |
	%	%	%	%
Expects to receive:				
More than the full amount	51	46	38	48
The full amount (not more or less)	30	36	34	32
Less than the full amount	15	15	24	16
Don't know	4	3	4	4
Weighted N (=100%)	557	223	99	880

student made even more difference to the likelihood of getting financial help from parents than Table 2.5 suggests. Excluding those living with their parents, among students whose parents were expected to make a contribution, 57 per cent of under-19s expected to receive more than the full amount compared to 33 per cent of 20–24 year olds. Conversely, 11 per cent of under-19s expected to receive less than the full amount compared to 23 per cent of 20–24 year olds.

After age 25, parental income was no longer taken into account in assessing the size of the maintenance grant, and students were unlikely to receive much financial help from parents. In fact, only 5 per cent of mature students received regular financial contributions from their parents, compared to 58 per cent of students under 25. It is not surprising therefore that the model showed a sudden increase at age 25 in the likelihood of taking out a loan.

After age 30, however, the likelihood of taking out a loan declined again, and students aged 35 and over were no more likely to take out a loan than 18 year olds. One possible explanation for this is that students embarking on courses when they were already in their 30s may have been less confident than younger students of receiving a financial return on new qualifications, and so have been generally less willing to incur debts in order to study. Another factor may be that older students received more financial help from spouses or partners. For all students in our data set who were aged 30 or over when they started their course (including those with no partner), the mean annual income of their partners was £6873. The corresponding figure for students of all ages was £991.

Other possible explanations for the declining propensity to take out a student loan after age 30 are a greater use of savings, greater earnings from casual or part-time employment, a greater incidence of employer sponsorship, or a greater use of commercial sources of credit. However none of these hold good. Older students were *less* likely to draw on savings than younger students (21 per cent of students aged 30 and over at the start of their course drew on savings compared to 43 per cent of the sample as a whole). The mean earnings during the academic year of students aged 30 and over were very close to the average for all students (£622 compared to £625). Although older students were slightly more likely than younger students to have employer sponsorship, the difference was very small (3 per cent of those aged 30 and over at the start of their course compared to 1.5 per cent of the sample as a whole). Finally, as we shall see in Chapter 3, commercial credit was not generally used as an alternative to student loans: on the contrary, students who used commercial sources of credit were more likely than other students to take out student loans.

Although eligibility for a student loan was independent of both parental and spouse's income, the value of the maintenance grant received from official sources was a strong predictor of the likelihood of taking out a loan.[20] In our data, students receiving no maintenance grant formed 30 per cent of the sample, and they were taken as the reference category against which to compare the effects of receiving grants of different sizes. In order to get an even distribution of respondents in each size band, the value of the grant was divided into deciles, each representing 10 per cent of the sample.[21]

---

20. The amount received as maintenance grant was calculated for the academic year 1995/96. It included both statutory and discretionary grants from Local Education Authorities (LEAs) in England and Wales, and grants from the Scottish Office Education and Industry Department (SOED) or Student Awards Agency for Scotland (SAAS) in Scotland and the Education and Library Board (ELB) in Northern Ireland. The total received was the sum of the amounts actually received for the autumn and spring terms 1995/96 plus the amount that the student expected to receive for the summer term. Allowances for special circumstances (single parents' allowance, disabled students' allowance, two homes allowance, older students' allowance, dependants allowance and extra weeks' attendance allowance) were included in the total. Grants from Access or Hardship Funds, and any other grants, awards bursaries or scholarships were not counted. There was missing information on the total maintenance grant received for 94 respondents..
21. The smallest grants (£1–£796) formed the fourth decile because students receiving no grant at all accounted for 30 per cent of the sample.

The results show that (with one exception) students who received a maintenance grant were more likely to take out a loan than those who did not.[22] However the relationship between the size of the grant and the likelihood of taking out a loan was not linear. The band £1651–£2340 (deciles seven to nine) included most students receiving the maximum grant, and these students were more likely to take out a loan than those whose grants were smaller (£1–£1650, or deciles four to six).[23] Within these two broad bands, there was no evidence that the likelihood of taking out a loan increased with the size of the grant. Students receiving grants of more than £2340 (decile ten) were less likely to take out a loan than students with grants of £1651–£2340, but more likely to do so than students with grants that were smaller than this. Grants of more than £2340 usually included special allowances such as the older students' allowance or the dependants allowance, which presumably meant that there was less need for a loan.[24]

As the size of the grant depended on the income of the student's parents or partner, the amount received was also a good proxy for family socio-economic circumstances. When the value of the maintenance grant was excluded from the model, the socio-economic group (SEG) to which the student belonged was a significant predictor of the likelihood of taking out a loan.[25] However, as Johnes (1994) found in his study of students at Lancaster University, once the value of the grant was included as a predictor variable, SEG lost its significance. In the present model, SEG

---

22. The exception was the sixth decile, where the estimate did not reach significance. This may have been a chance fluctuation.

23. In the academic year 1995/96 the basic maximum grant for students not living with their parents was £2340 in London and £1885 elsewhere. The basic maximum for students living with their parents was £1530.

24. See footnote 20. One possible factor affecting the relationship between the size of the maintenance grant and the likelihood of taking out a student loan could be whether or not students' parents gave them the full assessed contribution towards their maintenance. However there appears to have been little relationship between the size of the grant and the generosity of parents. Among students whose parents were expected to make a contribution to their maintenance, 32 per cent of those who received no maintenance grant expected to receive the full amount from their parents and 47 per cent expected to receive more than the full amount (weighted base N=292). For students with a grant of £1–£796 the corresponding figures were 29 and 46 per cent (base N=153); for students with a grant of £797–£1382 they were 32 and 50 per cent (base N=162); and for students with a grant of more than £1382 they were 35 and 50 per cent.

25. In the Student Income and Expenditure Survey, SEG is based on parental occupation (at student's age 16) for students aged under 26 at the start of their course and students aged 26 or more who had never been in paid work before the start of their course. For other students SEG is based on their main job before starting their course.

was dropped and the value of the grant retained as the latter was a better predictor of the likelihood of taking out a loan.[26]

If students were mature, that is, aged 25 or more when they started their course, then parental income was not taken into account in assessing grant entitlement.[27] This means that for mature students, the value of the maintenance grant received was not a proxy for the socio-economic circumstances of the family in which they grew up. Thus the relationship between the value of the grant and the likelihood of taking out a loan may have been different for mature and non-mature students. To test this, we fitted terms for the interaction between age and size of grant, and as there was a very large number of possible combinations of these two variables, these interaction terms had to be simplified. Model 1B in Table 2.1 gives the results.

The results suggest that students with big grants were more likely to take out a loan than students with no grant, whatever their age. Conversely, they also suggest that mature students were more likely to take out a loan than 18-year olds, whatever the size of their grant. However, for mature students, there was virtually no difference between those with a big grant and those with a relatively small grant in the likelihood of taking out a loan.[28] This contrasts with the results for younger students, where those with a big grant were much more likely to take out a loan than those with a small grant.

---

26. With gender, age, ethnicity, course length and year of study already fitted in the model, fitting SEG as a predictor produced a reduction in scaled deviance of 15.68 for the loss of five degrees of freedom while fitting the value of the grant produced a reduction of 61.06 for the loss of eight degrees of freedom. This means that adding in the value of the grant improves model fit more than SEG does.

27. For students aged 25 and over, grant entitlement depended on spouse's income (if they were married) and on any independent income they possessed. Parental income was also ignored for students aged under 25 in the following circumstances: the student had been married for at least two years at the start of the course; he/she had been supporting him/herself for at least three years before the start of the course; the parents were elderly or disabled; the student had been or was in care; the parents could not be contacted; main household income depended on a step-parent or guardian. Students whose grant did not depend on parental income were known as 'independent' students. In the Student Income and Expenditure Survey, about 9 per cent of students said that, although they were under 25, their parents' income was not assessed for grant purposes. This included about 3 per cent who had been self-supporting for three or more years, but very few (0.2 per cent) who had been married for two or more years.

28. Expressed in terms of relative odds, the odds of a mature student with a grant of £1650 or less taking out a loan were more than three times as great as the corresponding odds for a mature student with no grant (odds ratio = 3.03). The parallel odds ratios were 1.52 for students aged 18 at the start of their course, 1.21 for those aged 19, and 0.84 for those aged 20–24.

These results suggest that mature students getting relatively small grants were more likely than younger students to maximise their loan income. A plausible explanation for this is that younger students were more likely to get help from their parents, in the form of money, other gifts, and free board and lodging during vacations. In addition, older students may have expected a higher standard of living than their younger classmates, especially if they had previously worked full-time.

Factors that Made no Difference to Loan Take-up

In addition to the variables already discussed, a number of other possible predictor variables were tested, but found to have no significant effect on the likelihood of taking out a loan. For some of these, this was probably because their effects were already incorporated in the value of the maintenance grant. Thus for example, the length of the academic year was not significant, but an allowance was payable if the students had to attend their course for more than a certain number of weeks. Similarly, for students who were living with a spouse or partner, the partner's employment status made no significant difference. This may be because in many cases the partner's income was already taken into account in calculating grant entitlement.

The lack of significance of certain other variables is more surprising. One factor which we would have expected to influence the likelihood of taking out a loan was the expected level of future earnings, on the assumption that students who expected their future earnings to be high may have been more willing to go into debt in order to fund their studies. Though the Student Income and Expenditure Survey did not ask about expected future earnings, other variables may act as proxies for this. One such variable is the type of institution attended, in that students from high status institutions tend to have lower unemployment rates after completing their course than other students.[29] However, no significant

---

29. For 9.5 per cent of first degree graduates from Universities Funding Council (UFC) Universities in 1992, the first destination was believed to be unemployment. For other higher education institutions, the corresponding proportion was 13.5 per cent. This was despite the fact that 26 per cent of first degree graduates from UFC Universities went on to more full-time education or training, compared to 15 per cent of first degree graduates from other higher education institutions. 36.8 per cent of UFC first degree graduates had permanent UK employment as their first destination compared to 37.4 per cent of first degree graduates of other higher education institutions — a difference of only 0.6 per cent, despite the much greater

relationship was found between type of institution and the likelihood of taking out a loan.[30]

A second possible proxy for expected future earnings is the subject studied, as both graduate employment rates and the occupational level of employment after graduation vary with degree subject.[31] In his study of Lancaster University students, Johnes (1994) found that those on vocational courses were more likely to take out a loan than others. However subject of study is correlated with course length, and in our models subject is a significant predictor of loan take-up only if course length is not included in the model. Even then its significance is only marginal (10 per cent level of probability), and the effect is in the opposite direction from that predicted, with vocational students being less likely than others to take out a loan.[32]

Thus the present study provides no evidence that the likelihood of taking out a loan is affected by expectations of future earnings. However it

---

proportion of UFC graduates going on to more full-time education or training. (Figures are calculated from Higher Education Statistics Agency (1995), Table 22. They refer to England and Scotland only, as no figures for other higher education institutions in Wales and Northern Ireland were available at the time of writing.)

30. Type of institution was classified in two different ways. The first contrasted the 'old' universities with universities which had until recently been polytechnics and with other institutions of higher education that do not have university status. The second was based on Higher Education Funding Council's league tables arising from their 1996 research assessment exercise, which allocated a specific score to each institution. Neither classification even approached significance as a predictor of the likelihood of taking out a loan.

31. The known first destinations (at December 1995) of all UK domiciled students obtaining first degrees in 1995 (including those whose first destination was unknown) included the following: permanent employment 29 per cent; further study or training 17 per cent; unemployment 8 per cent. Two contrasting subject areas illustrate the variation between subjects. For students of business and administrative studies the figures were: permanent employment 43 per cent; study or training 7 per cent; unemployment 8 per cent. For creative arts and design the figures were: permanent employment 18 per cent; study or training 14 per cent; unemployment 10 per cent. Among all graduates entering paid, full-time permanent employment, 75 per cent took jobs in Groups 1–3 of the Standard Occupational classification, namely managers and administrators, professional occupations, and associate professional and technical occupations. Again, there was much variation between subject areas: for example, computer science 89 per cent; mathematical sciences 84 per cent; business and administrative studies 70 per cent; creative arts and design 60 per cent; humanities 55 per cent. (Figures calculated from Tables 2f and 4f, Higher Education Statistics Agency 1996).

32. The classification of subjects as vocational or non-vocational is to some extent a matter of judgement, and different classifications may produce different results. In the present study, the following are classed as vocational: medicine/dentistry/health; subjects allied to medicine; agriculture, forestry and veterinary science; computing; engineering and technology; architecture, building and planning; business and administrative studies; education.

must be stressed that this highly tentative finding is based on very inadequate proxies for future earnings.

Two further possible predictor variables were tested but proved insignificant. The region of the UK in which the higher education institution is located affects living costs while a student and possibly also expectations of future earnings. However this variable was not related to the likelihood of taking out a loan.[33] Secondly, it might be argued that parents who have experienced higher education themselves might be more generous in the financial support they offer their children, thus lessening their need for a loan. However parental possession of a degree was not a significant predictor of loan take-up, even when neither socio-economic group nor the value of the maintenance grant were included in the model.

Illustrative Estimated Probabilities

Annex A explains how the model estimates are interpreted as the multiplicative effects of the predictor variables on the odds of taking out a loan. However Table 2.6 gives an interpretation of the model results which may be intuitively more meaningful. It shows the percentage probabilities of taking out a loan that are estimated by the model for students with particular sets of characteristics, and how these change if one characteristic is varied while the others are held constant. It has to be stressed that Table 2.6 is illustrative only. The effect of a change in a given characteristic on the estimated percentage probability of taking out a loan depends on the particular combination of characteristics specified, and the number of possible combinations is very large indeed.[34]

In Table 2.6 we start with a student who is in the base or reference category of all the predictor variables; that is a white male in the first year of a three-year course in an institution outside Greater London, aged 18 at the start of the course, receiving no maintenance grant, with no partner and no children. For such a student, the estimated probability of taking out a loan is 39 per cent. The effects of changes in these characteristics are shown only if the model indicates that the difference is statistically

---

33. Two versions of this variable were tested, the first distinguishing all 12 standard regions and the second contrasting the more prosperous regions of London and the South East with the rest of the UK. Note that we have no data on where students lived before they entered higher education.
34. In contrast, the multiplicative effect on the odds of taking out a loan is constant for each factor, regardless of the values of the other predictor variables (unless interaction terms are specified in the model).

Table 2.6 *Probabilities of taking out a student loan estimated by Model 1A for students with specified characteristics*

(a) Men

Ethnic identification	Course length & year of study	Family situation	Age at start of course	Value of maintenance grant	Estimated probability %
White	yr 1 of 3 yr course	no partner/no children	18	no grant	39
Asian	"	"	"	"	20
White	yr 2 of 3 yr course	"	"	"	48
"	yr 3 of 3 yr course	"	"	"	49
"	1 yr course	"	"	"	17
"	yr 1 of 3 yr course	"	19	"	45
"	"	"	20	"	47
"	"	"	30–34	"	51
"	"	"	"	under £797	47
"	"	"	"	£797–£1382	53
"	"	"	"	£1651–£1872	65
"	"	"	"	£1873–£1976	63
"	"	"	"	£1977–£2340	64
"	"	"	"	£2341+	56
"	yr 3 of 3 yr course	"	25–29	£1651–£1872	85

continued

Table 2.6 *continued*

(b) Women

Ethnic identification	Course length & year of study	Family situation	Age at start of course	Value of maintenance grant	Estimated probability %
White	yr 1 of 3 yr course	no partner/ no children	18	no grant	31
Asian	"	"	"	"	15
White	yr 2 of 3 yr course	"	"	"	39
"	yr 3 of 3 yr course	"	"	"	40
"	1 yr course	"	"	"	13
"	yr 1 of 3 yr course	"	19	"	37
"	"	"	20	"	39
"	"	"	25–29	"	47
"	"	"	30–34	"	43
"	"	"	18	under £797	38
"	"	"	"	£797–£1382	44
"	"	"	"	£1651–£1872	56
"	"	"	"	£1873–£1976	55
"	"	"	"	£1977–£2340	56
"	"	"	"	£2341+	47
"	"	no partner/ has children	"	no grant	59
"	yr 3 of 3 yr course	"	25–29	£1651–£1872	93

Note: All estimated probabilities are for students outside Greater London.

significant, part (a) of the table giving the estimates for men and part (b) for women. Thus if the student described above were Asian rather than white, his estimated probability of taking out a loan would fall to 20 per cent. If the student were white but female, the estimated probability would be 31 per cent.

The last row of part (a) of the table shows the characteristics of male students with the highest estimated probability of taking out a loan (assuming that male students are unlikely to be lone parents). These are white students in the third year of a three-year course, aged 25–29 and receiving a grant in the range £1651–£1872; their estimated probability of taking out a loan is 85 per cent.[35] As the last row of part (b) of the table shows, women with similar characteristics but who are also lone parents have an estimated probability of taking out a loan of 93 per cent.

Model 2: *Taking out a Student Loan at any Time During the Course*

The findings presented so far relate to the likelihood of taking out a student loan during 1995/96, the academic year in which respondents to the Student Income and Expenditure Survey were interviewed. This was chosen as the main focus of analysis as much of the information in the survey relates specifically to that year. Another possible approach is to model the likelihood of taking out a loan at any time during the course up until the time of interview, including loans taken out both in 1995/96 and in earlier years. This dependent variable has the advantage of being perhaps a better measure of the propensity to take out a student loan, but the disadvantage that students' circumstances may have changed between the date when they took out a loan and the date of interview.

In fact, as Table 2.7 shows, the results of modelling the likelihood of taking out a loan at any time during the course were very similar to the results of modelling take-up during 1995/96 only (see Table 2.1). The main difference was exactly as we would predict, namely that the effects of course length and year of study were stronger. In particular, the likelihood of having taken out a loan was now significantly higher for students in the second, third or higher years of a course lasting four or more years than

---

35. The estimated probabilities for otherwise similar male students with grants of £1873–£1976 and £1977–£2340 are very similar.

for students in the first year of a three-year course. The effects of age at the start of the course were also stronger, with the difference between students aged 18 at the start and those aged 16–17, 21, and 22–24 now reaching significance. Another factor that was insignificant in Models 1A and 1B but significant in Models 2A and 2B was having a partner and dependent children, which increased the likelihood of ever having taken out a loan. In addition, studying in Greater London appeared to reduce the likelihood of taking out a loan, though only at a marginal level of significance. This may be because London students were more likely to live with their parents during term-time than students studying elsewhere (24 per cent of London students lived with parents or other relatives, compared to 13 per cent of students elsewhere).

Nearly all other variables that were insignificant as predictors of the likelihood of taking out a loan in 1995/96 were also insignificant as predictors of the likelihood of taking out a loan at any time during the course so far. There was one exception to this: a very detailed breakdown of subject of study into 20 disciplines produced an improvement in the fit of the model that was significant at the 5 per cent level of probability. This appeared to be largely because students of the physical sciences (such as physics and chemistry) and of the social sciences (such as economics, sociology, psychology) were more likely to take out a loan than others. However, more aggregated versions of the subject variable failed to produce significant results, and the vocational/non-vocational dichotomy was also insignificant. It is difficult therefore to interpret the model results for subject of study, and the significant coefficients for the physical and social sciences may have represented chance fluctuations.[36]

---

36. If we accept the 5 per cent level of probability, on average one in twenty model coefficients will be significant purely by chance.

Table 2.7 *Models for taking out a student loan at any time during the current course (excluding causally ambiguous predictors)*

	Model 2A estimate	Model 2B estimate
Constant	0.65	0.63
Gender:		
Male	1.00	1.00
Female	****0.67	****0.67
Ethnic identification:		
White	1.00	1.00
Black Caribbean, Black African, Black other	1.07	1.14
Asian (Indian, Pakistani, Bangladeshi, Chinese)	****0.42	****0.42
Other	1.47	1.50
Course length and year of study:		
1st year of a 3 year course	1.00	1.00
2nd year of a 3 year course	****1.96	****1.95
3rd year of a 3 year course	****2.44	****2.46
1 year course	**0.31	**0.33
1st year of a 2 year course	1.52	1.45
2nd year of a 2 year course	1.23	1.29
1st year of 4+ year course	0.73	0.73
2nd year of 4+ year course	**1.55	**1.54
3rd year of 4+ year course	*1.54	1.42
4th or higher year of 4+ year course	****2.96	****3.04
Family situation:		
No partner and no dependent children	1.00	1.00
Has partner but no dependent children	1.29	1.22
Has partner and dependent child(ren)	**1.93	1.52
Has dependent child(ren) but no partner	***3.85	***3.26
Location of HE institution:		
UK excluding Greater London	1.00	1.00
Greater London	*0.74	*0.73
Age at start of course:		
18	1.00	—
16–17	*0.64	—
19	***1.45	—
20	**1.64	—
21	*1.60	—
22–24	*1.60	—
25–29	***2.18	—
30–34	1.43	—
35 and over	0.93	—

continued

Table 2.7 *continued*

	Model 2A estimate	Model 2B estimate
Value of maintenance grant for 1995/96 (inc allowances):		
£0 (30% of sample)	1.00	–
4th decile (£1–£796)	1.29	–
5th decile (£797–£1382)	**1.45	–
6th decile (£1383–£1650)	1.02	–
7th decile (£1651–£1872)	****2.52	–
8th decile (£1873–£1976)	****2.74	–
9th decile (£1977–£2340)	****2.53	–
10th decile (£2341 or more)	****2.39	–
No information	***2.26	–
Age at start of course combined with value of maintenance grant:		
Age 18; no grant	–	1.00
Age 18; £1–£1650 (deciles 4–6)	–	1.31
Age 18; £1651 or more (deciles 7–10)	–	****2.79
Age 19; no grant	–	*1.45
Age 19; £1–£1650 (deciles 4–6)	–	**1.84
Age 19; £1651 or more (deciles 7–10)	–	****4.06
Age 20–24; no grant	–	***2.25
Age 20–24; £1–£1650 (deciles 4–6)	–	1.33
Age 20–24; £1651 or more (deciles 7–10)	–	****4.48
Age 25+; no grant	–	1.07
Age 25+; £1–£1650 (deciles 4–6)	–	***3.13
Age 25+; £1651 or more (deciles 7–10)	–	****3.82
All aged <18, regardless of size of grant	–	0.98
All with no data on size of grant	–	****2.93
N (unweighted)	*1950*	*1950*
Scaled deviance	*2317*	*2320*
Residual df	*1916*	*1919*

Significance levels: * 10%, ** 5%, *** 1%, **** 0.1%.

Chapter 3 | Models for Loan Take-up: Stage Two

In this chapter we explore the relationship between the take-up of student loans and additional predictor variables whose causal relationship with loan take-up is ambiguous. By this we mean that it is equally possible that the relationship with these factors resulted from a prior decision about whether or not to take out a loan, as that these factors themselves influenced the loan decision. Indeed, in some cases the relationship may have arisen because both the loan decision and its correlate were the joint product of some third factor which was causally prior. Thus the interpretation of the findings in this chapter is uncertain.

The analysis is restricted to student loans in the academic year 1995/96, the year of the survey, as data for most of the additional factors that we examine relate specifically to that year.

Including these additional predictor variables in our model of loan take-up changes the relationship between loan take-up and some of the predictor variables already discussed in Chapter 2. In order to show this, Table 3.1 includes the results of the earlier Model 1A alongside the results of the new Model 3F. Model 3F was built up in stages, and the effects of including the new variables on the relationship between our original predictor variables and loan take-up is seen more clearly when these stages are shown. Thus Table B.1 in Annex B gives the results for the interim models 3A to 3E .

The first of the causally ambiguous predictor variables to be included in the model is the type of accommodation in which the student lived during term.[37] Students who lived with parents or relatives had

---

37. More specifically, the type of accommodation occupied during the autumn term of 1995/96. Although a few students changed their type of accommodation between the autumn and spring terms, we chose to use the autumn term data as more student loans were taken out then than in the spring term.

Table 3.1 *Model for taking out a student loan in the academic year 1995/96 (including causally ambiguous predictors)*

	Model 1A estimate	Model 3F estimate
Constant	0.63	1.03
Gender:		
Male	1.00	1.00
Female	****0.70	***0.72
Ethnic identification:		
White	1.00	1.00
Black Caribbean, Black African, Black other	0.97	1.42
Asian (Indian, Pakistani, Bangladeshi, Chinese)	****0.40	0.66
Other	1.83	**2.93
Course length and year of study:		
1st year of a 3 year course	1.00	1.00
2nd year of a 3 year course	**1.45	0.98
3rd year of a 3 year course	***1.53	0.88
1 year course	**0.33	**0.27
1st year of a 2 year course	1.56	1.27
2nd year of a 2 year course	1.10	0.87
1st year of 4+ year course	0.71	0.77
2nd year of 4+ year course	0.99	0.71
3rd year of 4+ year course	0.99	0.72
4th or higher year of 4+ year course	1.27	*0.66
Family situation:		
No partner and no dependent children	1.00	1.00
Has partner but no dependent children	1.12	0.84
Has partner and dependent child(ren)	1.56	1.38
Has dependent child(ren) but no partner	***3.22	**2.85
Location of HE institution:		
UK excluding Greater London	1.00	1.00
Greater London	0.87	1.23
Age at start of course:		
18	1.00	1.00
16–17	0.68	1.23
19	**1.32	1.20
20	*1.43	*1.50
21	1.50	1.53
22–24	1.14	1.23
25–29	***2.02	***2.34
30–34	*1.69	**2.05
35 and over	1.08	1.20

continued

Table 3.1 *continued*

	Model 1A estimate	Model 3F estimate
Value of maintenance grant for 1995/96:		
£0 (30% of sample)	1.00	1.00
£1–£796 (4th decile)	*1.41	*1.40
£797–£1382 (5th decile)	***1.78	***1.96
£1383–£1650 (6th decile)	1.14	1.33
£1651–£1872 (7th decile)	****2.95	***2.00
£187 –£1976 (8th decile)	****2.73	*1.53
£1977–£2340 (9th decile)	****2.88	***1.91
£2341 or more (10th decile)	***2.00	1.20
No information	***2.11	1.54
Accommodation:		
Provided by college	–	1.00
Lives with parents or other relatives	–	****0.33
Rented or owned by student/other	–	1.18
Parental contributions 1995/96:		
£0 (41% of sample)	–	1.00
£1–£340 (5th decile)	–	0.86
£341–£750 (6th decile)	–	**0.63
£751–£1190 (7th decile)	–	**0.60
£1191–£1786 (8th decile)	–	***0.54
£1787–£2700 (9th decile)	–	****0.47
£2701 or more (10th decile)	–	***0.47
Commercial credit 1995/96:		
£0	–	1.00
Under £250	–	***1.55
£251–£500	–	****2.53
over £500	–	****2.80
No information	–	1.77
Term-time employment:		
No paid work during term-time	–	1.00
Paid work during term-time	–	1.15

continued

Table 3.1 *continued*

	Model 1A estimate	Model 3F estimate
Non-essential expenditure 1995/96:		
Under £819 (1st decile)	–	1.00
£819–£1168 (2nd decile)	–	1.08
£1169–£1440 (3rd decile)	–	1.18
£1441–£1667 (4th decile)	–	1.08
£1668–£1854 (5th decile)	–	*1.56
£1855–£2075 (6th decile)	–	***2.20
£2076–£2342 (7th decile)	–	**1.80
£2343–£2675 (8th decile)	–	****2.41
£2676–£3162 (9th decile)	–	****2.78
Over £3162 (10th decile)	–	****2.88
No information	–	0.91
Knowledge of student loans:		
Five questions correct	–	1.00
Four questions correct	–	****0.43
Three questions correct	–	****0.18
Two questions correct	–	****0.08
Less than two questions correct	–	****0.03
N (unweighted)	*1945*	*1945*
Scaled deviance	*2463*	*2021*
Residual df	*1911*	*1884*

Significance levels: * 10%, ** 5%, *** 1%, **** 0.1%.

substantially lower accommodation costs than students living either in accommodation provided by their college or in accommodation which they rented or owned independently. They thus had less need of a student loan, but they also may have chosen to live with their family in order to avoid going into debt. College accommodation also tends to be cheaper than accommodation rented on the open market, but college accommodation is not offered to all students. Model 3F in Table 3.1 shows that, compared to students in college accommodation, students who lived at home were much less likely to take out a student loan. Moreover, Table B.1 in Appendix B shows that, as long as non-essential expenditure during 1995/96 is not included as a predictor variable, students in college provided accommodation were less likely to take out a

Table 3.2 *Type of accommodation, by length of course and year of study*

	College provided %	Parents or relatives %	Rented or owned by student/other %	Weighted N = 100%
3 year courses:				
Year 1	49	16	35	*364*
Year 2	8	12	80	*374*
Year 3	12	10	78	*436*
Courses of 4 years or longer:				
Year 1	55	21	24	*175*
Year 2	9	18	73	*201*
Year 3	10	18	72	*91*
Years 4+	11	14	75	*212*
All students (including 1- and 2-year courses)	22	15	63	*1970*

Note: Sample numbers were not big enough to give the breakdown for students on one-year or two-year courses. There was missing information on accommodation for one respondent.

student loan than students in accommodation that they rented or owned independently.[38]

Once type of accommodation is included in the model, the effect of year of study on the likelihood of taking out a loan becomes much weaker. Table 3.2 shows the reason for this is that type of accommodation and year of study were closely related. First-year students were a little more likely than others to live at home, and much more likely than other students to live in college accommodation.

The next variables to be included in the model represent sources of student income other than maintenance grants and student loans. The first of these was the amount of financial support actually received from parents during the academic year 1995/96.[39] This variable is causally ambiguous

---

38. A survey of undergraduates at the University of Newcastle upon Tyne in 1992/93 also showed housing costs to be significantly associated with the total amount of debt held by students (including both student loans and other forms of credit) (McCarthy and Humphrey 1995).

39. This includes both the amount received to date at the time of interview in the spring term 1995/96, plus the amount that the student expected to receive during the rest of the academic year. It refers to the amount that parents actually gave, regardless of whether this was more or less than the contribution assessed for grant purposes.

because in some cases parents may have given their child more than their assessed contribution specifically to avoid the need for the student to take out a loan, while in other cases, students may have been forced to take out a loan because their parents gave them less than the assessed contribution. As with the value of the maintenance grant, the value of parental contributions is divided into deciles, each representing 10 per cent of the sample.[40]

In general, the greater the amount of money that parents gave their child, the less likely the student was to take out a loan. Note that this is after taking into account the value of the student's maintenance grant, which was itself directly related to the size of the contribution that parents were expected to make towards maintenance.[41] The value of the maintenance grant becomes less important as a predictor once actual parental contributions are included in the model, though it remains significant (see Table B.1). The fact that both variables are significant underlines the fact that parents' actual contributions to their child's maintenance often differed substantially from the contributions they were expected to make, as Table 2.5 has already shown.

A second possible source of student income is credit from commercial sources, such as bank overdrafts. Our model shows that the amount of commercial credit incurred by students during the academic year was strongly related to the likelihood of taking out a student loan.[42] Here, however, the relationship was the opposite of that for parental contributions: the greater their commercial debts, the more likely students were to take out a student loan. The causal link between these two variables was probably that they were the joint outcome of the student's circumstances and preferences. While both forms of borrowing were likely to arise out of financial need, the association between them also suggests that some students were willing to go into debt, while others tried to avoid debt if they possibly could.

---

40. As just over 40 per cent of the sample said they received nothing from their parents, the next lowest band (£1–£340) represents the fifth decile.

41. Except of course in the case of students classed as 'independent' for grant purposes – see footnote 27.

42. This includes all forms of commercial credit, including bank overdrafts, other loans, credit card debts and hire purchase, overdrafts being by far the most common. Figures include the actual amount of debt incurred by the time of interview in the spring term, plus the amount that the student expected to incur during the rest of the academic year.

Table 3.3 *Commercial credit during the academic year 1995/96, by age at start of course*

	£0 %	£1–£250 %	£251–£500 %	£501+ %	*Weighted N* =100%
Under 18	72	17	9	2	71
18	55	16	17	12	833
19	49	15	19	17	374
20	42	14	18	26	137
21	50	15	17	18	78
22–24	47	7	18	28	119
25–29	45	16	17	22	109
30–34	52	14	12	22	94
35 and over	60	11	13	16	116
All students	52	15	17	16	1931

Note: There was missing information on commercial credit for 39 respondents.

Once commercial credit is included in the model, age at the start of the course loses some of its strength as a predictor of loan take-up (see Table B.1). This is because, as Table 3.3 shows, up to the age of 20 the amount of commercial credit incurred by students was correlated with age. One reason for this is that some banks fix personal credit limits partly on the basis of age.

A third source of income is term-time employment. Comparison of the 1995/96 Student Income and Expenditure Survey with the parallel 1992/93 survey shows that there has been a big increase in student employment over the last few years (Callender and Kempson 1996). However, contrary to what might be expected, term-time employment did not generally appear to be treated as an alternative to taking out a student loan. In fact, in the 1995/96 survey, students were more likely to take out a loan if they did paid work during term than if they did not.[43] When asked about their reasons for borrowing, only 2 per cent of students who had ever taken out a student loan said it was an alternative to paid work.[44] Conversely, among students who had not taken out a loan

43. 57 per cent of students who had a job during term-time took out a loan (weighted base N 794), compared to 52 per cent of students who had no paid term-time employment (weighted base N 1153).
44. Specifically, only two per cent of students who had taken out a student loan chose one of the following reasons as their main reason for doing so: 'I did not want to get paid work', 'I could not find a job', and 'My parents/partner did not want me to take a paid job'.

during 1995/96, only 5 per cent said their main reason for not borrowing was that they preferred to get paid work than to take on a loan.

If term-time employment is included in the model together with the predictor variables discussed so far, we find that students who did paid work during term-time were significantly more likely than other students to take out a loan (see Model 3D in Table B.1). However this significance disappears when further predictor variables are added (see below).

The next set of variables fitted in the model relates to expenditure during the academic year 1995/96. This is divided into 'essential' and 'non-essential' expenditure, following the definitions of the Student Income and Expenditure Survey.[45] The most important components of essential expenditure were accommodation costs and expenditure related to accommodation, such as household bills. As these depended on type of accommodation, and type of accommodation is already included in the model, it is not surprising that essential expenditure proves insignificant as a predictor of student loan take-up.[46]

However non-essential expenditure was strongly associated with the likelihood of taking out a student loan. Once non-essential expenditure during the academic year had passed the fourth decile (that is, is more than £1667), then the greater the expenditure, the greater the likelihood of taking out a student loan tended to be. Obviously, causality can run in either direction here. Students may have borrowed with the specific purpose of financing their spending, or conversely may have found that they were obliged to take out a loan though they did not originally intend to do so, because of the amount that they had already spent.[47]

When we controlled for the level of 'non-essential' expenditure, the difference in take-up between students in college-provided accommo-

---

45. As with other money amounts, this includes expenditure incurred by the date of the survey and expenditure that the student expected to incur during the rest of the academic year. The 1995/96 Student Income and Expenditure Survey defined essential expenditure as including spending on accommodation, food, utility bills and household goods, course expenses, travel to and from the place of study, and expenditure on dependent children. Non-essential expenditure was defined as including spending on entertainment, travel for leisure purposes, credit repayments, clothing, other purchases and incidentals. These definitions have been the subject of some debate.
46. When accommodation is dropped as a predictor variable, essential expenditure becomes a significant predictor.
47. McCarthy and Humphrey (1995) in their 1992/93 sample of undergraduates at the University of Newcastle upon Tyne also found that leisure spending was significantly associated with the total amount of debt (from both student loans and other sources) that students had incurred.

dation and students who rented or owned independently disappeared. This suggests that the high rate of loan take-up among students in independent accommodation was linked with higher expenditure on other items. The coefficients for some other variables also changed. The effect of term-time employment on the likelihood of taking out a loan became weaker, and its significance fell to the marginal 10 per cent level. The amount of commercial credit also lost some of its strength as a predictor of loan take-up, though it remained highly significant. The reduction in the coefficients for these two variables suggests that, for some students, spending patterns may have created a need to maximise income.

The final predictor variable we included was the level of knowledge about student loans.[48] As Table 3.1 shows, this was extremely strongly associated with loan take-up – the less that students knew, the less likely they were to take out a loan. However in the large majority of cases, causality almost certainly ran in the opposite direction. Everyone who applied for a full-time place in higher education was sent a booklet explaining their entitlement to student loans, and the details were likely to be read much more carefully by those who intended to apply for one than by those who did not.[49] In addition, students who applied for a student loan had their knowledge of the scheme reinforced by the application form and by the loan or credit agreement which they subsequently had to sign. It is therefore hardly surprising if they ended up knowing more about the scheme than students who had not taken out a loan.

In all previous stages in the development of Model 3F, Asian students remained significantly less likely than other students to take out a loan (see Models 3A to 3E in Table B.1). However, once knowledge of student loans was included in the model, the difference between Asian and white students lost its significance. Moreover, ethnic identification was the only demographic variable that was changed in this way: the effects gender, family situation and age were all largely unaffected by the inclusion of knowledge as a predictor. This suggests that a lack of a detailed understanding of how student loans work may have been one reason for the low take-up rates among Asian students.

---

48. This variable is the number of questions (out of five) about student loans that the respondent answered correctly. A sixth question was also asked in the survey, but no account was taken of this in calculating knowledge scores as we deemed the question to be misleading.

49. The publications of the Student Loan Company are in fact the source that students most commonly used for information on student loans, and also the source most likely to lead to them being fully and accurately informed (Callender and Kempson 1996).

| Models for the Amount Borrowed

Maximum Loans in 1995/96

The total cost to the exchequer of student loans depends not only the number of students who take out loans, but on the amount of money that they borrow. This chapter explores the factors related to the latter.

Although under the system in force in 1995/96 student loans were not means-tested, the maximum amount that students could borrow in any one academic year depended on their circumstances. Table 4.1 shows the maximum amounts for the year in which the Student Income and Expenditure Survey was conducted. Students studying in London could borrow more than those studying elsewhere; students living with their parents could borrow less than others. The maximum loan was lower in the final year of the course as it did not cover the summer holiday in that year. Students were able to borrow less than the maximum amount if they

Table 4.1 *Maximum student loans in 1995/96*

	Full year	*Final year*
Students living away from their parents' home and studying:		
In London	£1695	£1240
Elsewhere	£1385	£1010
Students living at their parents' home	£1065	£ 780
Special rate*	£1530	£1240

* London students living away from their parents' home but receiving the 'home' rate of grant because it was deemed that they could live with their parents and still attend their course. The special rate no longer exists.

Table 4.2 *Maximum loans for which students were eligible*
(students who took out a loan in 1995/96)

Maximum loan:	Number of students (%)
£780 (living with parents; final year)	3
£1010 (living away from parents; outside London; final year)	30
£1065 (living with parents; full year)	5
£1240 (living away from parents; in London; final year)	5
£1385 (living away from parents; outside London; full year)	46
£1695 (living away from parents; in London; full year)	11
Weighted N (=100%)	966

Note: For 85 students it was not possible to determine the maximum loan for which they were eligible. In most cases this was because it was unclear when they applied for the loan.

wished. If they did so, they could not top up their loan later in the year, as only one loan application could be made in each academic year.

Table 4.2 shows the proportion of students taking out loans in 1995/96 who, as far as we can tell, were eligible for these different maxima. There is some uncertainty about these figures. Maximum loans depended on where students were living at the time they applied, but students may have later moved to a different type of accommodation. Although we know where students mainly lived during term, it is possible that this was different at the time they made their loan application.[50] In addition it was not possible to identify students who were eligible for the 'special rate' of loan. However, if the figures in Table 4.2 are correct, then three-quarters of students who took out loans in 1995/96 fell into two groups: those who were eligible to borrow £1385 (46 per cent), and those who were eligible to borrow £1010 (30 per cent).

Because the maximum loan for which students were eligible varied with circumstances, there is not much interest in modelling the actual amount borrowed – this was largely a simple function of their circumstances. Of more relevance is whether they borrowed the maximum

50. In fact, we only know whether they lived with their 'parents or other relatives apart from spouse'. We have treated all these students as if they lived with their parents, but if, for example, they lived with an aunt and uncle, their maximum grant would have been higher. If students took out their loan in the autumn term, we have based the maximum on where they lived in the autumn term, and if they took out their loan in the spring term, we have based the maximum on where they lived in the spring.

Table 4.3 *Percentage of maximum loan applied for*
(students who took out a loan in 1995/96)

Applied for:	Number of students (%)
Less than 50%	1
50%–74%	4
75%–93%	7
94%–99%	21
100% (or more)	67
Weighted N (=100%)	966

amount for which they were eligible, or whether they borrowed only a proportion of this. Unfortunately, determining this was not straightforward. As we have just seen, there was some uncertainty over the relevant maximum amount. In addition, there are also some data problems regarding the amount borrowed. For example, it is clear that students often rounded the amount that they said they had applied for to the nearest £100,[51] while in other cases, digits seemed to have been transposed or extra zeros added. There is a further complication in that the survey asked students how much they had applied for, not how much they had received. This of course may have been different, especially if borrowers had miscalculated their maximum loan. In fact about one in six of all students said they had applied for more than the amount for which they appeared to be eligible, and in the present analysis we have treated these as if they had borrowed the maximum.

However, the more serious problem in modelling the proportion of the maximum loan that students borrowed is that the variable has very little variance. As Table 4.3 shows, two-thirds of students who took out loans in 1995/96 borrowed the maximum amount or (apparently) more. A further fifth borrowed between 94 and 99 per cent of the maximum amount, and nearly all of these seemed to have rounded down the amount they said they applied for to the nearest £100. Thus in the present analysis students who borrowed between 94 and 99 per cent of the maximum are treated as if they had borrowed the maximum. This leaves only 12 per cent of all

---

51. For example, 65 students whose maximum loan appeared from their circumstances to be £1010 said that they had applied for £1000.

Table 4.4 *Models for whether borrowed the maximum amount in the academic year 1995/96 (students who took out a loan in 1995/96)*

	Model 4A estimate	Model 4B estimate
Constant	4.69	11.55
Maximum loan eligible for:		
£780 (living with parents; final year)	1.00	–
£1010 (away from parents; outside London; final year)	***4.27	–
£1065 (living with parents; full year)	2.55	–
£1240 (away from parents; in London; final year)	2.51	–
£1385 (away from parents; outside London; full year)	1.27	–
£1695 (away from parents; in London; full year)	0.80	–
Course length:		
3 years	1.00	–
1 or 2 years	1.31	–
4 or more years	*0.66	–
Course length and year of study:		
1st year of 3+ year course	–	1.00
2nd year of 3+ year course	–	***0.40
3rd year of 3+ year course	–	1.07
4th or higher year of 4+ year course	–	1.27
1 or 2 year course	–	0.99
Value of maintenance grant for 1995/96 (inc. allowances):		
£0 (30% of sample)	1.00	1.00
4th–6th deciles (£1–£1650)	**0.56	*0.62
7th–8th deciles (£1651–£1976)	0.78	0.85
9th–10th deciles (£1977 or more)	*2.05	*1.87
No information	2.34	1.79
Type of institution:		
Pre-1992 non-UFC institution	1.00	1.00
pre-1992 UFC university	*1.45	1.31
Age at start of course:		
Under 25	1.00	1.00
25 and over	0.72	1.09

continued

Table 4.4 *continued*

	Model 4A estimate	Model 4B estimate
Partner's annual income:		
No partner/no income/no information	–	1.00
£10,500 or less	–	0.94
above £10,500	–	***0.26
Knowledge of student loans:		
Five questions correct	–	1.00
Four questions correct	–	0.85
Less than four questions correct	–	***0.39
N (unweighted)	979	979
Scaled deviance	667	669
Residual df	965	964

Significance levels: * 10%, ** 5%, *** 1%, **** 0.1%.

borrowers in 1995/96 who borrowed less than the maximum, and it seems likely that there are data errors for some at least of this 12 per cent.[52]

With this very skewed distribution, it is best when fitting our statistical model to treat the dependent variable as a binary indicating whether or not borrowers applied for the maximum loan. However, even with a binary dependent variable, we are unlikely to get many useful results, as the proportion of the sample not applying for the maximum was so small. Table 4.4 shows our model results, but we stress that the models are in many ways unsatisfactory and the results are in no way conclusive. The sample for the models consists only of students who took out a loan in 1995/96.

Model with Unambiguous Predictors

In Model 4A in Table 4.4 we use mainly predictor variables whose causal relationship with the dependent variable was relatively unambiguous.[53] Having said this, the first predictor variable is the maximum loan that the

---

52. Students may have been encouraged to take out maximum loans because they could make only one loan application in each academic year. If they borrowed more than they found that they needed, they could repay the difference with no penalty. If, however, they borrowed less than they found that they needed, they could not go back to the Student Loan Company for the difference.
53. See Chapter 3 for a discussion of causal ambiguity.

student was eligible for. This incorporates information on accommodation, which, as discussed in Chapter 3, could itself sometimes be a consequence of a prior decision about whether or not to take out a loan. Nevertheless this variable must be fitted as a predictor in the model as it is a design variable, in the sense that any errors in the computation of the maximum loan will produce errors in the dependent variable.

Taking students living with their parents and in their final year (maximum loan £780) as the base or reference category, only one group of borrowers had a significantly greater probability of taking out the maximum loan. These were borrowers at institutions outside London who were living away from their parents and in their final year (maximum loan £1010). As noted earlier, maximum loans in the final year were smaller than in the preceding years. It may be that for students living away from their parents, final year maximum loans were lower in proportion to living expenses than maximum loans in earlier years. This interpretation is supported by the fact that the coefficient for final year London students living away from their parents is also positive and quite large, though the coefficient does not reach significance because sample numbers are very small. Alternatively, the result may simply reflect the fact that rounding errors are easier to spot for students whose maximum loan was £1010 than for others.[54]

As the variable for the maximum loan already incorporates a distinction between the final year and earlier years, we could not fit a separate predictor variable for year of course. However the length of the course was marginally significant, with borrowers on courses lasting four or more years apparently less likely to take the maximum loan than students on three-year courses. This may be because they were concerned about the total debt they would have incurred by the end of their course.

The value of the borrower's maintenance grant also had some effect on the amount borrowed. Compared to borrowers receiving no maintenance grant, those with relatively small grants (£1650 or less) were less likely to take out the maximum loan. At the other extreme, borrowers with relatively large grants (£1977 or more) appear to have been more likely to take out the maximum loan, though this result was only marginally significant. These results may reflect the degree of financial need amongst borrowers.

---

54. See footnote 51.

The final factor that may have increased the likelihood that a borrower took out the maximum loan was attendance at an 'old' university, defined as an institution funded by the UFC before 1992. However, once again this result was only marginally significant. As discussed in Chapter 2, no relationship could be found between attendance at an 'old' university and the likelihood that the student took out a loan at all.

Chapter 1 of the report explained the technical reasons why variables used to construct the weighting matrix for the survey data have been included as predictors in our models. In Model 4A, variables relating to studying in London and to year of study are incorporated into the variable for the maximum loan. The other weighting variable relating to age at the start of the course is fitted separately, but is not significant.

Model with Causally Ambiguous Predictors

When we attempted to include causally ambiguous predictors in our model for whether or not borrowers had taken out the maximum loan, it proved impossible to construct a satisfactory model. When further predictor variables were included in the model, the standard errors of the coefficients for the different categories of the maximum loan applied for become extremely large, so the results were not interpretable. One reason for this is that several categories of the 'maximum loan' variable had very small sample numbers.

For this reason, Model 4B in Table 4.4 uses an alternative specification. Instead of fitting separate predictor variables for the maximum loan (which incorporates a distinction between the final year and earlier years) and for course length, it fits a combined variable for course length and year of study, as sample numbers are more evenly distributed across the categories of this variable. With this specification, standard errors fall to more reasonable levels.

The results of Model 4B suggest that borrowers in the second year of a course lasting three or more years were less likely to take out the maximum loan than those in their first year. This may have been because they were starting to become concerned about the total amount of debt that they were accumulating. Coefficients for other causally unambiguous predictors were relatively unchanged, though attendance at an 'old' university lost its (marginal) significance.

Only two of the causally ambiguous predictors examined appeared to be associated with the likelihood of taking out the maximum loan. Student borrowers who had a partner with an annual income above £10,500 were less likely to take out the maximum loan than those with no partner or whose partner had no income. This result probably reflects the fact that borrowers with partners in better paid jobs were less likely than others to be in financial need.

The second causally ambiguous predictor that reached significance was the level of knowledge about student loans.[55] Borrowers who were relatively poorly informed about student loans were less likely to take out the maximum loan. The reasons for this are a matter for speculation. It may simply reflect a lesser degree of interest in the details of a scheme on the part of borrowers whom it affected less. Alternatively, it may reflect an erroneous assumption on the part of those taking out less than the maximum loan that they could borrow the balance later in the year.

---

55. See Chapter 3 for details of how knowledge of student loans was measured.

Chapter 5 | Reasons for Borrowing and Not Borrowing

So far we have examined the take-up of student loans from a very objective point of view, exploring the factors that were statistically associated with the decision to take out a loan. In this chapter we look at the decision from the student's perspective.

Respondents to the 1996 Student Income and Expenditure Survey who took out a loan either in 1995/96 or earlier were asked why they had done so, and offered a list of alternatives from which to choose their answer. Those who gave more than one reason were asked which was the most important. Similarly, students who had never taken out a loan were asked why they had not done so. Unfortunately, an error in the questionnaire meant that first-year students who had not taken out a loan were not asked why, though first-years with loans were asked their reasons for borrowing.

In our analysis we group reasons for taking out a student loan into three categories: financial need, financial advantage, and other reasons.[56] Reasons for not taking out a loan are grouped into: no financial need, concerns about borrowing, and other reasons.[57] We look at how these

56. 'Financial need' included the following reasons: 'I did not want to get paid work', 'I needed the money', 'I could not find a job' and 'My parents/partner did not want me to take a paid job'. 'Financial advantage' covered the following reasons: 'I wanted to buy a particular item' and 'Cheap way to borrow money/tax efficient'. 'Other' reasons included: 'My parents/partner encouraged me to get one' and 'I thought I had to in order to get Access Funds', plus reasons that could not be fitted into any of the above categories.

57. 'No financial need' included the following reasons: 'I do not need the money' and 'Still using up a loan taken out in a previous year'. 'Concerns about borrowing' included: 'I prefer to get paid work than take on a loan', 'I do not like borrowing money', 'My parents/partner did not want me to', 'I was concerned about the repayments' and 'I was reluctant to take on a further debt'. 'Other' reasons included: 'I prefer to borrow from other sources', 'I did not think I was eligible for another loan', 'I prefer to get an overdraft', 'Do not have a bank/building society account', plus reasons that could not be fitted into any of the above categories.

Table 5.1 *Main reason for taking out a student loan, by various characteristics (all students who had ever taken out a loan)*

	Main reason for taking out a loan:			
	Financial need	Financial advantage	Other	Weighted N = 100%
Gender:				
Male	75	16	9	585
Female	78	10	11	565
Age at start of course:				
Under 19	73	16	11	477
19	74	11	15	226
20–24	84	11	4	217
25 and over	80	13	7	229
Year of study and length of course:				
1 or 2 year course	75	10	15	66
Year 1 of 3+ year course	72	16	12	279
Year 2 of 3+ year course	75	14	11	339
Year 3 of 3+ year course	81	13	6	332
Year 4+ of 4+ year course	80	11	9	135
Maintenance grant 1995/96:				
No grant	68	19	13	262
Up to £1650	71	16	13	290
£1651 – £1976	87	6	7	260
£1977 and over	80	13	7	273
All borrowers	77	13	10	1150

Note: Percentages do not always sum to 100 because of rounding error.

reasons for borrowing and not borrowing were related to factors that were important as relatively unambiguous predictors of the likelihood of taking out a loan (see Chapter 2). Unfortunately, for two of these factors – ethnic identification and family situation – sample numbers in the key categories of interest were too small for cross-tabular analysis, and so these variables are not discussed here.

By far the most important reason for taking out a loan was financial need, which was cited as the main reason for their decision by more than three in four borrowers. A further one in seven referred to the financial advantages of student loans, and one in ten gave other reasons. In contrast, by far the most important reason for not borrowing was

Table 5.2 *Main reason for not taking out a student loan, by various characteristics (students in second and higher years who did not take out a loan in 1995/96)*

| | Main reason for not taking out loan: | | | |
	No financial need	Concerns about borrowing	Other	Weighted N = 100%
Gender:				
Male	32	56	12	*213*
Female	21	68	11	*306*
Age at start of course:				
Under 19	30	62	8	*276*
19	26	61	13	*97*
20 and over	17	66	16	*146*
*Year of study and length of course:**				
Year 2 of 3+ year course	29	64	7	*229*
Year 3 of 3+ year course	22	63	15	*192*
Year 4+ of 4+ year course	24	60	16	*75*
Maintenance grant 1995/96:				
No grant	34	56	10	*205*
Up to £1650	26	65	9	*154*
£1651 and over	15	70	15	*140*
All non-borrowers	26	63	11	*519*

* No data are available for first year students or students on one-year courses. Sample numbers are too small to show percentages for second year students on two-year courses. Percentages do not always sum to 100 because of rounding error.

'concerns about borrowing', cited by nearly two in three non-borrowers, with 'no financial need' cited by another one in four and other reasons by one in ten.

Tables 5.1 and 5.2 show that there were small but consistent differences in the reasons that men and women gave for their decision. Men were more likely than women to cite financial advantage as their main reason for taking out a loan, while women were more likely than men to say that they had not got a loan because of concerns about borrowing, and less likely than men to say that 'no financial need' was the reason. This supports our suggestion in Chapter 2 that the gender difference in loan take-up was due at least in part to differences of personality and socialisation.

The tables also show that students who were aged 20 or more when they started their course were more likely than younger students to cite 'financial need' as their reason for getting a loan, and less likely to cite 'no financial need' as their reason for not borrowing. This again confirms our earlier suggestions for why older students had a relatively high take-up rate.

Broadly speaking, the further on students were in their course, the more likely they were to cite 'financial need' as their main reason for borrowing, and the less likely they were to cite 'no financial need' as their reason for not borrowing. This accords with our earlier finding that students in the second or third year of their course were more likely to take out loans than first-year students.

The relationship between the reasons for the loan decision and the size of the maintenance grant was also broadly as expected. Students receiving no maintenance grant, who usually came from more prosperous families, were the group least likely to say that they had taken out a loan because of financial need, and were also the group most likely to cite 'no financial need' as their reason for not borrowing. In contrast, students with grants over £1650 showed the opposite pattern of response.

Chapter 6 ▍Discussion

Scope of the Analysis

In this final chapter we highlight some of the more important results of our analysis, and discuss some of their possible implications. First, however, we need to be clear about the scope of our work.

The aim of this analysis was to explore the individual factors associated with the take-up of student loans. Some of our findings are relevant to the wider debate on the funding of higher education, but the general question of how higher education should be funded is well beyond our brief.

Note also that our work is concerned only with the take-up of loans from the Student Loan Company. Students quite commonly take out loans of other kinds, notably bank overdrafts, but we do not deal with these except in so far as they relate to student loans. Our study was carried out at a time when student loans were designed to help with living expenses, within a system in which means-tested maintenance grants of roughly equal value were also available, and where the government paid the tuition fees for all home students on designated courses. Patterns of take-up will undoubtedly change now that maintenance grants are to be replaced by loans.

As described in Chapter 1, when the Student Loans scheme was introduced in 1990, maximum loans were relatively small in relation to full maintenance grants. In the following years, in accordance with the policy outlined in the 1988 White Paper (Cm 520), maximum loans were increased while the value of the full maintenance grant fell in real terms. By 1996/97 maximum loans and grants were almost equal. It follows that the students who took part in the 1995/96 Student Income and Expenditure Survey could not incur as much student loan debt as students who began their courses in 1996/97. Levels of debt will almost certainly increase much more as a consequence of the latest changes to student funding. The total amount of debt is very relevant when considering the impact of loan repayments on students' future disposable incomes.

An important limitation of our work was the absence of data on a crucial element in students' decisions about whether to take out a loan. Although the 1995/96 Student Income and Expenditure Survey has very good data on many relevant factors, it was designed to cover students' current financial circumstances, and did not collect information on their expectations about their future earnings. However if taking out a loan is in part an investment decision, then the expected financial return to higher education is highly pertinent. Average returns accruing to graduates as a whole are relevant, but not sufficient for understanding the loan decision, as returns are likely to vary with the subject studied, the institution attended, examination results, the occupation that the student is planning to enter, and the student's own personal characteristics. The proxies used in Chapter 2 are very inadequate substitutes for proper measures of expected future earnings, and questions on the latter should be included in any future survey of student finances.

Although the statistical models showed associations between the decision to take out a loan and a wide range of factors, the nature of the association was often far from clear. In many cases, causality could run in either or both directions, or the loan decision and the factors associated with it could be the joint result of other factors which we may or may not have measured. In our modelling, we tried to distinguish factors which were clearly causally ambiguous from factors whose causal priority to the loan decision was less doubtful. However, there were very few factors indeed, other than gender and ethnic identification, that could not possibly be influenced by a prior attitude to student debt. This difficulty in interpreting our findings makes it hard to use them to predict future levels of loan take-up. The Student Income and Expenditure Survey is cross-sectional, giving a snapshot of student finances at one moment in time. A longitudinal study would be necessary to determine the true causal relationships of some factors with loan take-up, and even then, the task would not be easy.

Another area in which our analysis is weak is in the modelling of the amount borrowed. However, the reason for this weakness – the fact that the vast majority of student borrowers take out the maximum loan for which they are eligible – also means that at the moment this issue is of relatively minor policy interest.

Loan Take-up and Parental Resources

One of our most important findings concerns the relationship between the take-up of student loans and the financial circumstances of the student's family of origin. Our results show that the students with large maintenance grants were more likely than students with small grants or no grant at all to take out a student loan, and to borrow the maximum amount. They were also more likely to cite financial need as their main reason for borrowing. As for most students the size of the maintenance grant was inversely proportional to their parents' income, it follows that students from poorer families were incurring bigger debts than students from relatively prosperous backgrounds.

In theory this should not have happened. Student support for maintenance comprises two components, the grant and the loan, and parental contributions were assessed only in relation to the grant element of student maintenance. Thus the assessed contribution of wealthy parents whose child received no maintenance grant formed only part of the total help available from the full basic grant plus loan – this total being the amount that students were expected to need to live on. In practice, students with small grants or no grant at all were less likely to take out a loan than students with large grants, and this was almost certainly because many parents – nearly half of those who were assessed for a contribution – gave their child more than the assessed amount.

The question therefore arises of whether the prospect of incurring large debts might deter young people from poorer families from entering higher education. This question cannot be answered by the data presented in this report since they related only to men and women who were already in higher education. However, despite the rapid growth in participation in post-compulsory education in Great Britain in recent years, there remain marked social class differences in the likelihood that similarly qualified young people will continue their full-time education after 16 or enter higher education.[58]

---

58. See, for example, Payne, Cheng and Witherspoon 1996 and Egerton and Halsey 1993.

The need to examine the impact of funding arrangements on young people from less well off families is not peculiar to the Student Loans scheme – any scheme for transferring the costs of higher education from the state to the student will meet the problem that some parents will be more able and willing than others to subsidise their children's education. This difficulty must be balanced against the possibility that transferring more of the costs of higher education from the state to the student could release resources for other educational spending that might be of particular benefit to children from poor families, for example spending on state nursery and primary education.

Nevertheless, we need to explore how the potential deterrent effects of the loan system might be minimised. Under the scheme in place at the time our study was carried out, loan repayments began when the student's income after leaving higher education reached 85 per cent of national average earnings, and above this threshold, the size of repayments depended only on the size of the debt, not on the borrower's income. The burden of repayments was thus greatest for borrowers whose earnings were just above the repayment threshold, though the size of this burden for those at the threshold could appear very different depending on how the calculations are made.[59] Some commentators have argued that the potential deterrent effects of student loans on entry to higher education would be reduced if repayments depended more closely on income, and have proposed a range of schemes to achieve this end. The government's response to the recommendations of the National Committee of Inquiry into Higher Education accepts that repayments should be made on an income contingent basis.

Although the implications of the Student Loans scheme for students from poorer families need to be carefully considered, there is another group of students for whom the possibility of loan funding is of undoubted benefit. These are the students with parents who are expected to make a contribution to their maintenance, but who, for whatever reason, contribute less than the assessed amount or even nothing at all. Our data show that one in six students whose parents were expected to

---

59. For example, for a student who entered higher education in 1992, took out three maximum 'outside of London' loans, and started making repayments in April 1996, repayments took up 3.6 per cent of gross income at the repayment threshold (DfEE calculations). For a student who entered higher education in 1995, took out three maximum 'London' loans, and started making repayments in April 1999, repayments took up 10 per cent of net income (after deductions for tax and National Insurance) at the repayment threshold (Barr and Crawford 1996).

make a contribution faced this problem. The problem was most severe for students aged 20–24 at the start of their course, nearly one in four of whom received less than the assessed parental contribution. Under the system in force when our study was carried out, loans were not means-tested, and were an important source of funding for these students. Although the new loans will be means tested, there will be a limit on the amount of the loan that is means tested, so that all students will receive some support from the new loans.

Another issue raised by our findings concerns students who had well-off parents contributing more than the assessed amount, who were still taking out loans. This of course was no more than their right, as loans were not means-tested and one of the original aims of the Student Loans scheme was to shift part of the burden of student funding away from parents. Nevertheless the fact remains that some well-off students, who before the introduction of student loans would have received no state payments towards their maintenance, are now receiving such payments in the form of subsidised loans with zero real interest rates.

We found that nearly one in eight students who took out student loans said that the main reason for doing so was not financial need, but financial advantage. Indeed some students who did not need the loans for their living expenses invested the money in order to profit from the interest differential, while others used them to finance leisure spending or the purchase of large consumer goods. Some commentators have argued that a solution to this problem would be to end the interest rate subsidy for student loans.[60] If loans attracted commercial interest rates, there would be no incentive for students to take them out unless they were in financial need.

Lone Parents

Students who are also lone parents tend to have particularly severe financial difficulties. In an earlier report on the 1995/96 Student Income and Expenditure Survey, lone parents stood out as being under greater financial strain than most (Callender and Kempson 1996). Despite being eligible for Income Support, they were more likely than other students to be in arrears with their household bills and other regular commitments, and the total amount of their debts was much greater than for other students. It is therefore not surprising that our models have shown that lone parents were

60. See, for example, Barr and Crawford 1996.

more likely than other students to take out a student loan. For lone parents, qualifications have a special role as a route out of poverty and dependence on the state, because good earnings are needed if they are to be better off in work than on benefits (Ermisch and Wright 1992). We need therefore to pay attention to the degree to which current funding arrangements might encourage or discourage their entry to higher education.

Attitudes to Debt

The decision about whether to take out a student loan is not driven only by financial need or the perception of financial advantage. There appears to be a group of students who are averse to the idea of debt, however economically rational it may be to borrow.[61] Nearly two-thirds of students who chose not to take out a loan in 1995/96 cited concerns about borrowing as the main reason for their decision. In contrast, students who took out student loans also tended to borrow more than others from commercial sources of credit.

Our models suggest that women may be more averse to the idea of borrowing than men, and this gender difference also shows up in the reasons given for the loan decision. The models also suggest that Asian students may be more averse to the idea of borrowing than other students, though small sample numbers meant that we could not directly compare attitudes here, and lack of knowledge about how student loans work may also be involved.

Now that a much greater proportion of student finances is to come from loans, these negative attitudes towards borrowing may deter some groups of young people from entering higher education. Some people, drawing a distinction between borrowing to finance current consumption and borrowing to invest in the future, will see this as a problem of providing the appropriate education and publicity to encourage young people to change their attitudes. Others will see an issue of principle, being reluctant to encourage a culture that is unworried by debt.

---

61. The distinction between people who are averse to the idea of debt and those who use debt to manage their finances is found in other spheres outside of student life. For example, a study of families with children living on very low incomes found that some would go to great lengths in order to avoid borrowing or getting behind with bills, while others would regularly borrow in order to repay existing debts, thus ending up in multiple arrears (Kempson, Bryson and Rowlingson 1994).

References

Barr, N. and Crawford, I. (1996) *Student Loans: Where Are We Now?* Suntory and Toyota International Centres for Economics and Related Disciplines, London School of Economics. Discussion Paper WSP/127

Callender, C. and Kempson, E. (1996) *Student Finances: Income, Expenditure and Take-Up of Student Loans*. PSI Publishing, London

Cox, D.R. and Snell, E.J. (1989) *Analysis of Binary Data (2nd Edition)*. Chapman and Hall, London

Department for Education and Employment (1996) *Statistics of Student Loans in the United Kingdom – 1995/96*. Press Release 405/96

Department for Education and Employment (1997a) *Higher Education for the 21st Century*. Report of the National Committee of Inquiry into Higher Education

Department for Education and Employment (1997b) 'Government responds to Dearing Committee Report on Higher Education'. Press Release 226/97

Department of Education and Science (1988) *Top-Up Loans for Students*. Cm 520 HMSO, London

Egerton, M. and Halsey, A. (1993) 'Trends by social class and gender in access to higher education in Britain'. *Oxford Review of Education* Vol. 19, pp 183–196

Ermisch, J. and Wright, R. (1992) *Lone Parenthood and Employment: Male-Female Differences in Great Britain*. University of Glasgow Department of Political Economy. Discussion Papers in Economics No. 9214

Francis, B., Green, M. and Payne, C. (1993) *The GLIM System Release 4 Manual*. Clarendon Press, Oxford

Herbert, A. and Kempson, E. (1996) *Credit Use and Ethnic Minorities*. PSI Publishing, London

Higher Education Statistics Agency (1995) *Higher Education Statistics for the United Kingdom*. HESA, Cheltenham

Higher Education Statistics Agency (1996) *First Destinations of Students Leaving Higher Education Institutions 1994/95*. HESA, Cheltenham

Johnes, G. (1994) 'The determinants of student loan take-up in the United Kingdom'. *Applied Economics* vol. 26, pp 999–1005

Kempson, E., Bryson, A. and Rowlingson, K. (1994) *Hard Times? How Poor Families Make Ends Meet*. PSI Publishing, London

McCarthy, P. and Humphrey, R. (1995) 'Debt: the reality of student life'. *Higher Education Quarterly* vol. 49 pp 78–86

Payne, J., with Cheng, Y. and Witherspoon, S. (1996) *Education and Training for 16–18 Year Olds: Individual Paths and National Trends*. PSI Publishing, London

Steel, J. and Sausman, C. (1996) *Rate of Return to a Degree*. Paper presented to the Dearing Committee of Enquiry into Higher Education

Annex A ▌Interpreting the
Coefficients of the
Logistic Model

The model estimates are presented in the form of a multiplicative effect on the odds of taking out a loan. The base or reference category of each predictor variable is set to 1.00, and the effects of the other categories of the variable are assessed relative to the base category. Estimates less than 1.00 indicate a reduction in the odds of taking out a loan, and estimates greater than 1.00 indicate an increase. Thus for example, in Model 1A the odds of taking out a loan for women students are seven-tenths of the odds for men students. This, of course, is after controlling for all the other predictor variables included in the model. Similarly, for students who have at least one dependent child but no partner, the odds of taking out a loan are more than three times greater than the odds for students who had neither partner nor dependent children (again, after controlling for the other variables in the model).

The constant in the model represents the estimated odds of taking out a loan for a student who is in the base or reference category of each predictor variable; in Model 1A this means white male students in the first year of a three-year course, who were 18 when they began their course, receive no maintenance grant, have neither a partner nor dependent children, and are studying outside of London.

Note that we have talked about the *odds* of taking out a loan, not the probability. Odds are an alternative way of expressing probabilities; thus

$$\text{odds} = \text{probability}/(1\text{-probability})$$
and $\quad\text{probability} = \text{odds}/(1+\text{odds}).$

For example, if 75 students in a class of 100 took out a loan, then their probability of taking out a loan would be 0.75 or 75 per cent, but their odds of taking out a loan would be three to one on (3–1, or 3.00). If only 25 students in the class took out a loan, then their probability of taking out a loan would be 0.25 or 25 per cent, while their odds would be three to one against (1–3, or 0.33). It follows that to say that a particular characteristic halves the odds of taking out a loan is not the same as to say that it halves the probability of taking out a loan. In fact sometimes a large effect on odds represents a fairly small effect on probabilities, depending on the particular values involved. As some readers will be unaccustomed to working with odds ratios, in addition to presenting the model estimates, we illustrate the size of the effects of the predictor variables in the model by calculating the predicted probability of taking out a loan for students with specified combinations of characteristics.

Significance testing in the logistic model is carried out by adding new predictor variables one at a time and testing whether the term as a whole leads to a significant improvement in the fit of the model, conditional on the terms already included. The t-test approximates to this test, and can be used to see which specific categories of the predictor variable are doing the work. For example, in Model 1A, the variable indicating ethnic identification produces a significant improvement in the model fit, but only because Asian students are, as a group, less likely to take out loans than students belonging to other ethnic groups. Black students and students belonging to other ethnic groups are not significantly different from white students in this respect.

Annex B | Additional Tables

Table B.1 Model for taking out a student loan in the academic year 1995/96, including causally ambiguous predictors and showing the stages in which the model was built up

	Model 1A estimate	Model 3A estimate	Model 3B estimate	Model 3C estimate	Model 3D estimate	Model 3E estimate	Model 3F estimate
Constant	0.63	0.60	1.04	0.74	0.68	0.44	1.03
Gender							
male	1.00	1.00	1.00	1.00	1.00	1.00	1.00
female	****0.70	****0.67	****0.66	****0.67	****0.64	****0.68	***0.72
Ethnic identification							
White	1.00	1.00	1.00	1.00	1.00	1.00	1.00
Black Caribbean, Black African, Black other	0.97	1.10	1.01	0.93	0.94	1.04	1.42
Asian (Indian, Pakistani, Bangladeshi, Chinese)	****0.40	***0.44	***0.42	***0.42	***0.43	***0.47	0.66
Other	1.83	*1.97	1.88	*2.07	*2.18	*2.03	**2.93
Course length and year of study							
1st year of a 3 year course	1.00	1.00	1.00	1.00	1.00	1.00	1.00
2nd year of a 3 year course	**1.45	1.15	1.16	1.08	1.08	1.13	0.98
3rd year of a 3 year course	***1.53	1.22	1.26	1.07	1.08	1.15	0.88
1 year course	**0.33	**0.30	**0.33	**0.29	**0.28	**0.31	**0.27
1st year of a 2 year course	1.56	1.67	1.64	1.29	1.28	1.20	1.27
2nd year of a 2 year course	1.10	1.04	1.07	1.00	0.97	0.96	0.87
1st year of 4+ year course	0.71	0.75	0.75	0.79	0.80	0.81	0.77
2nd year of 4+ year course	0.99	0.80	0.82	0.82	0.81	0.83	0.71
3rd year of 4+ year course	0.99	0.81	0.81	0.73	0.72	0.76	0.72
4th or higher year of 4+ year course	1.27	1.05	1.07	0.86	0.87	0.90	*0.66

continued

Table B.1 *continued*

	Model 1A estimate	Model 3A estimate	Model 3B estimate	Model 3C estimate	Model 3D estimate	Model 3E estimate	Model 3F estimate
Family situation							
No partner and no dependent children	1.00	1.00	1.00	1.00	1.00	1.00	1.00
Has partner but no dependent children	1.12	0.92	0.91	0.97	0.98	0.89	0.84
has partner and dependent child(ren)	1.56	1.24	1.25	1.33	1.43	1.48	1.38
Has dependent child(ren) but no partner	***3.22	***2.75	**2.52	**2.55	***2.84	**2.31	**2.85
Location of HE institution							
UK excluding Greater London	1.00	1.00	1.00	1.00	1.00	1.00	1.00
Greater London	0.87	0.96	0.97	1.06	1.03	1.05	1.23
Age at start of course							
18	1.00	1.00	1.00	1.00	1.00	1.00	1.00
16–17	0.68	0.90	0.91	1.00	0.99	1.04	1.23
19	**1.32	**1.31	*1.30	1.25	1.24	1.19	1.20
20	*1.43	*1.41	1.34	1.16	1.14	1.25	*1.50
21	1.50	**1.71	1.51	1.50	1.46	1.42	1.53
22–24	1.14	1.21	0.99	0.91	0.90	0.87	1.23
25–29	***2.02	***2.12	*1.68	*1.72	*1.70	**1.81	***2.34
30–34	*1.69	*1.64	1.22	1.30	1.30	1.38	**2.05
35 and over	1.08	1.08	0.84	0.96	0.96	0.93	1.20

continued

Table B.1 *continued*

	Model 1A estimate	Model 3A estimate	Model 3B estimate	Model 3C estimate	Model 3D estimate	Model 3E estimate	Model 3F estimate
Value of maintenance grant for 1995/96							
£0 (30% of sample)	1.00	1.00	1.00	1.00	1.00	1.00	1.00
£1 – £796 (4th decile)	*1.41	**1.56	**1.51	**1.48	**1.47	**1.56	*1.40
£797 – £1382 (5th decile)	***1.78	****1.94	***1.77	***1.76	***1.75	***1.95	***1.96
£1383 – £1650 (6th decile)	1.14	**1.51	1.25	1.16	1.18	1.33	1.33
£1651 – £1872 (7th decile)	****2.95	****2.79	****2.09	****2.02	***2.02	****2.16	***2.00
£1873 – £1976 (8th decile)	****2.73	****2.50	***1.86	***1.61	**1.63	***1.78	*1.53
£1977 – £2340 (9th decile)	****2.88	****2.51	***1.88	***1.79	***1.79	***1.85	***1.91
£2341 or more (10th decile)	***2.00	**1.72	1.38	1.36	1.34	1.33	1.20
No information	***2.11	***2.23	***1.95	**1.83	**1.85	**1.88	1.54
Accommodation							
Provided by college	—	1.00	1.00	1.00	1.00	1.00	1.00
Lives with parents or other relatives	—	****0.48	****0.40	****0.45	****0.42	****0.30	****0.33
Rented or owned by student/other	—	****1.61	***1.56	***1.41	**1.36	1.21	1.18
Parental contributions 1995/96							
£0 (41% of sample)	—	—	1.00	1.00	1.00	1.00	1.00
£1 – £340 (5th decile)	—	—	0.79	0.87	0.89	0.81	0.86
£341 – £750 (6th decile)	—	—	**0.67	0.73	0.76	*0.69	**0.63
£751 – £1190 (7th decile)	—	—	**0.62	**0.62	**0.64	****0.57	**0.60
£1191 – £1786 (8th decile)	—	—	****0.59	***0.59	**0.60	****0.55	****0.54
£1787 – £2700 (9th decile)	—	—	****0.50	***0.51	***0.54	****0.47	****0.47
£2701 or more (10th decile)	—	—	***0.54	**0.58	**0.62	***0.54	***0.47

continued

Table B.1 *continued*

	Model 1A estimate	Model 3A estimate	Model 3B estimate	Model 3C estimate	Model 3D estimate	Model 3E estimate	Model 3F estimate
Commercial credit 1995/96							
£0	–	–	–	1.00	1.00	1.00	1.00
Under £250	–	–	–	****1.94	****1.91	****1.76	***1.55
£251 – £500	–	–	–	****2.69	****2.69	****2.60	****2.53
Over £500	–	–	–	****3.86	****3.81	****3.22	****2.80
No information	–	–	–	1.11	1.15	1.29	1.77
Term–time employment							
No paid work during term–time	–	–	–	–	1.00	1.00	1.00
Paid work during term–time	–	–	–	–	***1.33	*1.21	1.15
Non–essential expenditure 1995/96							
under £819 (1st decile)	–	–	–	–	–	1.00	1.00
£819 – £1168 (2nd decile)	–	–	–	–	–	1.26	1.08
£1169 – £1440 (3rd decile)	–	–	–	–	–	1.21	1.18
£1441 – £1667 (4th decile)	–	–	–	–	–	1.16	1.08
£1668 – £1854 (5th decile)	–	–	–	–	–	**1.71	*1.56
£1855 – £2075 (6th decile)	–	–	–	–	–	****2.24	***2.20
£2076 – £2342 (7th decile)	–	–	–	–	–	****2.20	**1.80
£2343 – £2675 (8th decile)	–	–	–	–	–	****2.37	****2.41
£2676 – £3162 (9th decile)	–	–	–	–	–	****3.23	****2.78
Over £3162 (10th decile)	–	–	–	–	–	****3.26	****2.88
No information	–	–	–	–	–	1.26	0.91

continued

67

Table B.1 continued

	Model 1A estimate	Model 3A estimate	Model 3B estimate	Model 3C estimate	Model 3D estimate	Model 3E estimate	Model 3F estimate
Knowledge of Student Loans (number of questions answered correctly out of five)							
Five correct	—	—	—	—	—	—	1.00
Four correct	—	—	—	—	—	—	****0.43
Three correct	—	—	—	—	—	—	****0.18
Two correct	—	—	—	—	—	—	****0.08
One or none correct	—	—	—	—	—	—	****0.03
N (unweighted)	1945	1945	1945	1945	1945	1945	1945
Scaled deviance	2463	2404	2388	2286	2279	2224	2021
Residual df	1911	1909	1903	1899	1898	1888	1884

Significance levels: * 10%, ** 5%, *** 1%, **** 0.1%.